More Like Old Times

Alan Coren

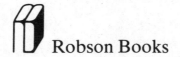

Robson Books

First published in Great Britain in 1990 by Robson Books Ltd,
Bolsover House, 5–6 Clipstone Street, London W1P 7EB

British Library Cataloguing in Publication Data
Coren, Alan *1938–*
  More like old times.
  I. Title
  828.91409

ISBN 0 86051 681 4

Typeset by Bookworm Typesetting, Manchester
Printed in Great Britain by
Butler & Tanner Ltd., Frome and London

Introduction

A Sense of History

Another year! Another deadly blow!
Another mighty Empire overthrown!
— William Wordsworth

Another year! Or maybe less!
What's this I hear? Well can't you guess?
— Edward Cantor

I t's all relative, really. Some pace the Kremlin corridors, some the maternity ward, but the footstep is roughly the same length and takes roughly the same amount of time to fall. If history is the essence of innumerable biographies — and this is neither the time nor the place to engage in a slanging match with Thomas Carlyle — it all comes down to what seemed important at the time.

I did not lose a bloc last year, nor become a father, big things, admittedly, both. But I became a tree and lost my Strangler Spindle, I had a sandpiper on my roof and a gorilla on my doormat, I acquired a murder weapon and a bucket of dung, I learned to play the ukulele and organized my burial at sea. I talked with the living dead, I kissed the boys and made them cry, I fought the Garrick Mafia and the Barnet Gestapo, I survived all that French barbers and British stonemasons could throw at me, and I took my rightful place, at last, in the gallery of Poland's great — while, upon the border of life's rich tapestry, fish, tortoises, frogs and jumping beans worked their curious counterpoint, tiny but arresting, like the Bayeux phalluses.

Not all of this, of course, took place in Cricklewood. Hayes, as you would expect, came into it, and Twin Falls, Idaho, and Corsica, and Cap d'Antibes; and the night my old man scooped up a shrunken Japanese head without even dropping his Lancaster into third gear means that the Far East also receives, however fleetingly, its due.

I think there's more, but you really can't expect me to remember everything. That, after all, is why I jotted it down in the first place.

AC

JUNE

Birdman of Cricklewood

I wish it would get lighter. I have every reason to believe there is a green sandpiper on my chimney. If this is indeed so, it could well be a first for Cricklewood. When word gets out, the streets will be full of anoraked ornithomaniacs with telescopes and tape recorders, building hides — though God knows what manner of hide would fox the Cricklewood fauna: a cardboard pillar box, perhaps, a canvas skip, an inflatable, prevandalized telephone booth.

For not only does the green sandpiper never appear in summer, its haunt is the margin of lakes and dykes, where it forages for molluscs. Since I have, as far as I know, a mollusc-free chimney, I can only induce that it is up there scanning for dykes.

That is probably why green sandpipers are not seen in summer. In summer they go out only at dawn in order to look for the margins of things to which they will repair in autumn to begin foraging. The green sandpiper is clearly a forward planner. Do not ask me how it can spot distant dykes at dawn; a glint of reflected moonlight, possibly, or a whiff of mollusc on the breeze.

The sky is, however, getting lighter. Any minute now, I may be in a position to confirm that it has the white rump which distinguishes it from the common sandpiper, provided it is not standing in such a way that the chimney obscures its rump.

Why am I so convinced, against all the odds, that it is a green sandpiper? Because it is going "kli-weet-a-weet". It has been going "kli-weet-a-weet" ever since I crept down here, at 3am, with my new *Observer's Book of Birds*.

I bought this on Saturday, because the current heatwave wakes me just before dawn every day, and I lie there staring at the ceiling, and then the birds begin hammering and tonging, so that there is naught for it but to grope downstairs and put the kettle on, and on Saturday I took the tea into the garden because it was cooler, and a million birds shrilled and clattered around me, and it was suddenly borne in upon me what an incompetent eavesdropper I was. I could not identify a single bird.

I have never been able to identify birds. Few townies can. We can generally distinguish between a sparrow and a pigeon on the grounds of size, but even then we have to see them together, to be certain. Starlings are a real headache: is that a big sparrow, we say, or a tiny pigeon?

So I hurried home from Waterstone's on Saturday, and I spent Sunday reading, and here it is, Monday dawn, and I am in a position to identify anything. I am soaking up the deckchair's dew and I have a tiny torch, and every time one bunch of feathers shouts at another one, I flip through the pages until I have got its number from the little paragraphs which describe the song. A doddle.

There was a Manx shearwater poking about in the acacia a while back. Why it thinks the acacia is a tunnel, it is not for me to say; it may well be that the flight from the Isle of Man has so knackered it that either its eyesight or its memory is shot, possibly both, but it was in there going "kuk-kuk-hoo-coo", so I knew it wasn't a knot (the knot is one of the birds I should always, now, be able to spot even without looking it up, because, according to page 84 of the *Observer's Book of*

10

Birds, it goes "knot", which is extremely considerate of it. If starlings went "starling", we should all know where we were.)

The ignorant among you may be puzzled about the tunnel reference. That is because you haven't shone your little torch on to page 20: "The Manx shearwater comes to land at breeding places at night, and shuffles to tunnels from which its sepulchral husky voice coos 'kuk-kuk-hoo-coo'."

It has now gone quiet, so it is probably breeding. The option would be that it is feeding, but I think this unlikely, since it lives on squid. I may know even less about octopods than I do about birds, but I'm pretty sure they don't hang out in acacia trees. If the shearwater wants breakfast, it will have to leg it back to the Isle of Man.

Damn. The green sandpiper has just quit the chimney. It's light enough to see it go, but not light enough to clock its rump. It wouldn't matter, but, as it flew, it seemed not to be going "kli-weet-a-weet". More like "weet-weet-weet". No "Kli" at all.

I bet it was only an osprey.

Local Derby

The house eructates, but discreetly. Not much rattles: a pane in a warped sash, a loose cistern-lid, a glass on a draining board.

"That'll help," says Henry.

"Should," corrects Henry's mate, cautiously.

"Should," nods Henry.

11

A long pause while they listen. Then, in a far intestinal fold, the house gurgles. There is also, somewhere, not a belch this time, but a susurration of gently expelled gas. I am embarrassed for the house, as if it were an elderly relative.

"See?" says Henry's mate. "Still there."

"Funny buggers," says Henry, "airlocks."

He feels the copper pipes, running his palm up and down them with surprising tenderness. His mate puts an ear to the flue, shakes his head, purses his lip.

"Have to bleed her again," says Henry.

His mate fingers a worn joint, examines his finger, sniffs it.

"Don't like this sweating."

"Or the breathing," says Henry. "She's breathing in at least two places, to my sure and certain knowledge. Definitely."

They are not plumbers at all, they are apothecaries. They go about their business not with a modern technician's manner, but with a medieval quack's listening and poking and smelling and licking and feeling, and murmuring a jargon not of breakdown but of malady. We are not standing in a Cricklewood boiler-room, we are standing in the belly of some sickly gargantua going down with terminal flatulence, as the result of an imbalance of humours. What is wrong with my central-heating system lies in the mystic relationship between air, fire and water. It can be only a matter of time before Henry's mate passes him a jar of leeches.

"The thing is," says Henry. "We are not getting hardly more than a drip from the header tank."

"I wouldn't even call it a drip," says his mate.

Henry, a kindly man, is irritated by this brusqueness. It is unseemly, at a sickbed. He turns, scowling.

"What would you bloody call it?" he says.

"I wouldn't call it bloody nothing," says his mate. "How do I know what you'd call something that isn't even a drip?"

"Pressure," explains Henry to me, "is what we're after. If we had a bit of pressure we'd be all right. Put a hose on down here, force the airlock back up."

They have been here since 10am. It is now after 3pm.

"I'll leave you to it," I say, not for the first time, and I crawl back up to the attic, and I stare at the keyboard for a bit, while, under my feet, the varicose pipework clunks and bongs arhythmically with the pitiful tappings of the two men buried far beneath my domestic ruins. Until, suddenly, there is a faint gargle from the radiator beside me, and a waft of unfamiliar warmth, like a dog's breath, and two pairs of boots clumping up the attic stairs, and a couple of heads in the doorway.

"Nice and warm, then?" says Henry, smugly.

"What did it?" I say.

"Wonderful thing, a bit of pressure," says Henry.

"He's got a telly up here and everything," says his mate.

"You've finished then?" I say, getting up, reaching for a wallet.

"Yes," says Henry.

"Mind you," says his mate, quickly, "they're funny things, airlocks. Not watching the Derby, then?"

"It's never 3.45?" cries Henry.

"What do you mean, funny things?" I say.

"They can form again right after you've bled 'em," says Henry's mate. "Am I right, Henry?"

"I shouldn't think you get much of a reception up here in the roof," says Henry, to me. "I should think you get a lot of interference."

I switch it on. Willie Carson is cantering Nashwan to the start.

"No chance," says Henry's mate. "Got to be Starkey's day."

"Swinburne and Stoute," says Henry. "Past the post. Cost two million as a yearling, Warrshan. Past the post."

"When will we know if the airlock's out for good?" I inquire.

"Hard to say," says Henry. "We're nice and near the tank up here, though. We'll hear her if she turns."

"Terimon looks a bit tasty," says his mate.

As I write, they are watching the start of the 4.40. Henry

13

likes the look of Restless Don. The heating's fine, but you can never tell with airlocks. They're funny things.

One Man and His Cog

Today we have the naming of parts. Yesterday we had little things falling out and rolling into the flower beds. And tomorrow we shall have what to do after the Council regrets that it is unable to treat scrap motor-mowers as normal household detritus within the meaning of the 1834 Refuse Act. But today, today we have the naming of parts. All of the other mowers are purring like bloody Ferraris in all of the neighbouring gardens, and today we have the naming of parts.

This is the Strangler Spindle and Pin Assembly. And this is the Strangler Flap, whose use I will see of, when I am given my Strangler Spindle. And this is the Split Pin for the Strangler Spindle, which in my case I have not got. As a matter of fact, I have not got the Strangler Flap, either, although I know exactly where it went when it flew off the Strangler Spindle, because I saw the small splash in the pond.

I would have gone after it, with the net that I use for dead orfes, had the rest of the mower not been falling to pieces around me, and had all of those pieces not seemed major, compared to a Strangler Flap or a Split Pin for the Strangler Spindle.

Or seemed so at the time. But, having rung ten mower

14

spares dealers, I now know that the Strangler Flap and the Split Pin for the Strangler Spindle are as major as you get. Or, rather, don't, because both bits in this case they have not got.

None of us has got a Strangler Spindle and Pin Assembly, either: what I was referring to in paragraph two was only the exploded illustration of the carburettor on page 19 of the Maintenance Manual, which in my case I *have* got. It bears scant relation, however, to the Exploded Carburettor itself, which in my case I have also got, because the Exploded Carburettor itself has fewer bits lying around it than it ought to have, according to the exploded illustration on page 19.

It does not seem to have a Split Pin for Tickler Stem, either, nor a Needle Seating. These may, though, not be in the pond. When the carburettor exploded yesterday, after the mower struck the acacia, not everything flew into the pond. Out of the corner of my eye, as I was endeavouring to retrieve what I then believed was a major part (because it was big, and smoking slightly), I noticed the leaves of a berberis being disturbed, as when a Split Pin for Tickler Stem flies through.

I have been under the berberis, though. I have even been under the berberis with a torch at 2am, but there is no sign of the Split Pin for Tickler Stem or the Needle Seating.

Today, just after dawn, I took all the retrievable parts of the Exploded Carburettor and laid them on the path, which is how I discovered there were fewer of them than there were in the exploded illustration on page 19. I did not know they were called anything, then, of course. I did not know what they were called until I telephoned the first of the dealers to explain that my carburettor had disintegrated, and we gradually established what I had not got.

"I have got the fat thing with a blob at one end and a spring," I would say.

And he would think, and reply: "That is the Tickler Stem and the Tickler Spring. Have you got a little tiny sort of a tin peg effort?"

And I would say: "No."

And he would say: "That is the Split Pin for the Tickler Stem."

But he had not got it, either. Nor the Strangler Spindle. Nor the Strangler Flap. None of them had, although one expects a Needle Seating any day now.

I have spent nine hours with the Yellow Pages and the telephone, and the rest of the neighbourhood mowers have fallen silent, because they have done their parallel lines and their owners are chuckling over their Pimm's. And now the sun is setting over my path and throwing long shadows of all of the little bits of my mower, and I can hear my grass growing, but I can do nothing about it. For today we have the naming of parts.

Thy Branches Ne'er Remember

It is Tuesday, and I am standing next to Neil Kinnock. From time to time, I nod deferentially towards him; occasionally, indeed, I bow quite low in his direction — some might say scrape — and, every time this happens, David Owen (rooted to a spot a few yards off) trembles violently.

Do not, however, rush to mark me down as just another time-serving hack in the process of rebuttering his daily bread: these obeisances have nothing to do with the fresh breeze blowing in from Europe. What they have everything to do with is the fresh breeze blowing in from Nuneaton. For here, in the sunny quadrangle of Higham Lane School, the

Leader of the Opposition is an ornamental cherry and I am a whitebeam. What David Owen is, though, remains, as ever, anybody's guess, since, as ever, his label is obscured.

We are, in short, trees. To be yet more punctilious, we are in short trees. Our identities are embodied in wispy saplings, dotted around the pupillary greensward in the company of our peers (not the least of which is Lord Lichfield). Others of our peers are soon to be enrooted: Germaine Greer is coming, and Bryan Gould, and Margaret Drabble, and Rachael Heyhoe Flint, a roster so disparate as to call to mind an Agatha Christie denouement in which those in the library are invited to wonder what they are doing here.

They are all, in this case, being 50 years old. That is because Higham Lane School itself is 50 years old, and its enterprising head, Alan Breed, has come up with the engaging wheeze of commemorating the milestone by inviting 50 quinquagenarians to dig a hole and plant themselves such immemoriality as aphids, acid rain, ozone perforations and future education policies permit. Which latter risk should silence nitpickers keen to point out that Neil Kinnock is a mere 47, and the Prime Minister — also invited — a sere 63: while Mr Breed claims he waived the age qualifications on the grounds of their eminence, I strongly suspect he was cannily hedging his bets against despoliation. Should educational support so further deteriorate that schools may one day be enjoined to hawk firewood to keep in business, the local authority axe might well pause before levelling something of the same political timber as itself.

Not, sadly, that his scheme has entirely worked. Mrs Thatcher is not coming. The head has received a letter stating that "the Prime Minister has no plans to visit Nuneaton", a phrase which suggests she has grown so paranoid as to treat any approach, however innocent, as a Parliamentary Question with an iron fist concealed inside it. She is doubtless even now girding her loins against a supplementary letter from Mr Breed, inquiring about the EMS.

For me, I could not wait to spring into gumboots and roar up the A5. Apart from anything else, Higham Lane School is not only my age, it is the age of my own old school, and I wanted to bang it with a tuning-fork and wallow in the hum. I was not disappointed: like mine, the school is a redbrick Cunarder beached in a playing field, an architectural style of which precious little remains, and every mottled pantile, every parquet oblong, every steel-girt transom and cream-painted corridor resonated with memory.

Even, I fancied, the group of boys and girls dragooned into arboreal service might have been my own contemporaries, frozen somehow in time; especially since Nuneaton seems to have maintained those modes for which the metropolitan parent yearns. They wear school uniforms, and listen patiently, with clean ears, and when they speak, they say "sir", and if they are upbraided for daring to run in a corridor, they do not drag sir around the corner and kick him witless.

They were even astonishingly restrained with the hose. It cannot be easy to be 14 years old, at the business end of the school's fire equipment and faced with a headmaster and his guest standing either side of a hole and shouting for irrigation. In the event, I got the whitebeam in with no more than a spattered sock.

Instant immortality. But as we trooped out of the quadrangle, I could resist neither a backward glance to where I and my generation nodded in the breeze, nor a wayward reflection, not on the last 50 years but on the next.

Will, I wonder, this tree continue to be, when there's no one about in the Quad?

18

Strings Attached

It was the best of presents, and the worst of presents. Furthermore, it also represented what is the best and the worst about all presents, which is that they define the giver's view of the recipient. Each birthday, in short, the gifties are gien us to see oorsels as others see us.

It was mine on Tuesday, though it pains me to write about it. Not because I care about evaporating time, but because my fingers hurt. As I type, I wince. Only from Left Hand Fingers 1 and 2, mind, but if you type the way I do, that represents a considerable input loss. It is like having half the workforce of one's little attic factory suddenly going sick. How shall we fulfil these work-norms, what is the expedient answer to our process problems, shall we re-tool, write shorter words, cut out adverbs entirely, what are the year-on-year budget implications if Left Hand Fingers 1 and 2 are permanently on the fritz? Especially as Right Forefinger is also somewhat below par, though not on its typing surface: it hurts only when I lift the coffee, but the way this factory operates, that is no small debility.

At least, though, there is an answer to the Right Forefinger problem. The answer is a felt pick. Don Ball says so, on page 6. He says that some people may have difficulty keeping Right Forefinger limp, in which case, they may be happier with a felt pick. Don Ball does not offer "felt pick" capital initials, because he clearly feels it cannot be anthropomorphized the way that Fingers can. Don Ball says Fingers are Friends.

19

I do not know what possessed my daughter to give me a ukulele, also Don Ball's seminal (but erroneously titled) work, *You Can Play The Ukulele*, plus *The George Formby Songbook*. Is she unsubtly saying it is time for me to hang up the Olivetti, twitch my mantle, and stride from the hill I am over as a hack to fresh woods and pastures new? Tonight, Bob says opportunity knocks for Lonnie Coren? A Uke, A Yuk, and A Maimed Left Hand?

Or is she simply expressing a cheering filial view of me as musical wag, life and soul, roll back the carpet, all together now, Oh If Women Like Them Like Men Like Those Why Don't Women Like Me?

That is why it was both the best and the worst of gifts. For while there is nothing I have longer dreamt of being than a bloke who could, when conversation flagged, whip a ukulele from his tail-coat and launch into *Leaning on a Lamp-post*, I was yesterday forced finally to face the fact that there was nothing I stood less chance of being. Yesterday was a bad day. I took the uke out of its case and I looked at it. It had four strings and 12 frets. I looked at *The George Formby Songbook*. Each chord had a little picture of the ukulele keyboard above it, with little black dots showing where you had to put your fingers.

I tried this.

After three hours, I reached a conclusion. You needed 48 Left Hand Fingers. The ukulele is an instrument for 12 players. In order to be the life and soul of a party, you have to be a team. It is like club cricket. Every Saturday, you meet outside The Rat & Cockle, and you go off to play your ukulele fixture. Never mind the songbooks and the felt picks, we should need blazers, ties, all that. How we should all get round one ukulele would, of course, be something of a problem, but I believe I have cracked it. I am not a complete musical ignoramus. You would need 12 ukuleles, and the players would fire in sequence, one man per pre-arranged chord, like bell-ringers.

It is the only alternative to being born with your little ukulele in your hand. Nobody of 51, once he has contorted his left hand into covering four frets, could be expected to move it to cover four different ones. Wrists don't grow that way. My chord is A7, whatever that means. It is the one which yesterday desquamated Fingers 1 and 2, and it was quite enough. All I shall ever be able to do is come in when the team gets to "I'll climb this blinking ladder till I . . ." and go out again so that the chap who does E7 can carry on with ". . . get right to the top".

Oh yes, and I can play one melody. I learned it when I had to tune the ukulele, and I telephoned a friend with an untin ear, and he sang the melody over the telephone while I twisted pegs until his ear was satisfied. The melody is *My Dog Has Fleas*.

The Bach Double Ukulele Concerto it ain't, but next time you're throwing a party, bear it in mind.

Adventures in the Skin Trade

The cow watched me as I slotted the car into the parking lot. It did not move until I had got out and locked the door. Then it lumbered up. "Welcome to the House of the Dead," said the cow.

I really didn't want this. Already apprehensive about what I was going to have to do inside, I was in no shape to handle unanticipated trouble outside. All along the North Circular Road I had been rehearsing what I was going to have to do inside, wondering whether I should shove my voice down an octave, whether I should grin as I spoke, or whether I should simply ignore utterly the nudgy conspiracy that the salesman

21

must have entered into (with a weary smile of his own) a hundred times before.

I knew that the salesman would say: "Are you looking for anything in particular, sir?"

And I knew that I should have to reply: "Yes, I'm looking for a little pouffe."

I had even gone to the preposterous lengths of looking up the word beforehand in the *Shorter Oxford* to see if there might perhaps be another word, but there wasn't. True, the *SOD* defined it as "a very soft stuffed ottoman or couch", but I wasn't going to say, "Yes, I'm looking for a very soft stuffed ottoman or couch", partly because that was not the sort of thing I could hear myself saying, but mainly because I was not looking for a very soft stuffed ottoman or couch, I was looking for a little pouffe. All the research taught me was that the blokes who cobbled the *SOD* together had never gone shopping, because if you are looking for a little pouffe but ask for a very soft stuffed ottoman or couch, the salesman will show you fifty large things you do not want before you are finally forced to explain to him that what you are looking for is a little pouffe, and he will ask you why you did not say so in the first place, and when he realizes why you did not say so in the first place, you will realize that you might as well have walked in grinning, nudged him in the ribs, dropped your voice to Chaliapin level and told him what you really wanted.

Oh, yes, I did learn something else from the research, which was that the derivation was onomatopoeic, and French XVIIIth century. It described what happened when an XVIIIth century Frenchman sat on a very soft stuffed ottoman or couch. This left me just enough time to wonder what happened when Frenchmen sat down on one prior to the XVIIIth century, and how they managed to communicate what happened to one another, before I got the car out and drove to Leatherland.

Where the cow was waiting in the carpark to ambush me.

Some Saturdays, it's a mistake to get up at all.

Leatherland – for those of the uninitiated who might have

assumed it was yet another theme park disneyed out of enterprise wasteland by some DTI-subsidized spiv with a view to providing Fun For All The Family, performing crocodiles for the kids perhaps, possibly a Krafft-Ebing Pavilion for the discerning fetishist – is in fact a huge furniture hypermarket just north of Hanger Lane.

"According to our estimates," said the cow, after I had made the mistake of asking it what it wanted (I had not unnaturally assumed that it was some kind of sales gimmick, possibly even offering a 10 per cent discount on little pouffes), "this establishment contains the flayed skins of two thousand animals."

"Probably nearer five," said the other end of the cow. I did not know what to say, so I said: "I'm not a vegetarian. I mean . . ."

"There is," said the front half of the cow, "all the difference in the world between eating your fellow animals because . . ."

"Even though we personally don't go along with it," said his rump.

". . . because you see that as a way of keeping yourself nourished, and ripping their skin off just to have something to sit on. Degradation is what that is."

"Worse than fur coats," mumbled the rump.

What made this exchange even more bizarre was that the cow, like all pantomime cows, had a big fixed grin on its face, through which all this sombre stuff was honking. And, as I made to walk past it, the grin said: "I mean, do you really *need* what you're going to buy? What is it?"

I thought for a moment. Just long enough.

"It's a very soft stuffed ottoman," I said. "Or couch."

JULY

Rags to Riches

At the cry, my heart leapt, and after it the gooseflesh and the neck-hairs. Not, you understand, from shock, nor from terror, nor even from that apprehension which might forgivably greet an unattributable bellow on a quiet suburban afternoon. What I was was, well, thrilled: for it was a stirring cry, though strange: not entirely mortal, yet not quite spectral either – rather, perhaps, the ambivalent efflux of an avatar's glottis.

"ERRENBOW!" it cried, time and again, "ERRON-BOW! ERRONBOW!" and the house-fronts gave the unfathomable echo back. But it was not merely the impenetrably runic syllables that set the adrenal cortex jangling, it was the sound of the song that bore them: a plangent note, yet compounded of both thunder and vibrato; shot through with challenge, yet plaintive; rich, yet somehow simultaneously chilling. The sort of a cry you would expect either (a) to greet a king from across the water hurling his stallion over the final ridge in reunion with his delirious people; or, alternatively, (b) to bid him stricken farewell as fate doomed him to desert them forever. All

27

depending upon whether he and the horse were getting larger or smaller.

Who, you said to yourself as the mullions rattled, is Errenbow? What his tribe and what his mission? Why is he coming back to Cricklewood, or quitting it? Is this some kind of sign?

So I went to the window.

Outside, grinding up the shallow gradient of our street, there was indeed a horse. At least, something which had undoubtedly been a horse once, though its current status might very well have sent the Jockey Club scuttling to their more recherché manuals. It was pulling, albeit inadequately, a cart yet more ancient than itself, and with even more bits sticking out of it at odd angles.

And standing in the back of the cart, the reins slack in his hands, stood a small scruffy man; who, as I watched, roared "ERRENBOW"!" again. Where he dredged the resonance from, God alone knew; he had no chest to speak of. His entire diaphragm would have fitted in Pavarotti's ticket-pocket. Nor, clearly, was he hailing anyone else; this was Errenbow himself.

I went to the front door, and opened it, and he reined in his horse and looked at me from beneath his ratty cap. The cart's flankboard read: *Nothing Reasonable Refused Best Prices Paid*.

"Got anything?" said Errenbow, in a perfectly normal voice.

In fact, I had. Like most normal men, I have a garage with an old bath in it, and a couple of spare wheels from forgotten cars, and a ladder with just enough rungs left to make you hesitate to chuck it on a bonfire, and a number of three-legged garden chairs – all those items with a jobsworth factor just below that required to interest dustmen.

So I opened the garage door, and Errenbow put a brick under his wheel and said something intimate to the shafted bonebag, and we went inside, and he banged about in the gloaming for a while, and finally he said: "This it, then?"

"Yes. Did you see the bath?"

28

"Got any onyx?" said Errenbow.

"What?"

"Onyx. Or marble. Slabs for preference, but I'll take table-tops."

"Those wheels," I said, "came off a V-registration Golf. The tyres are still good."

"Mahogany mantelpieces?" said Errenbow. "Brass door furniture, for example, period fingerplates? Chromium towel-rails, if original?"

"There's a ladder," I said.

"You haven't modernized, then?" said Errenbow. "You haven't chucked out original features?"

"No."

"Pity. They don't half shift, original features. You wouldn't believe the calls I get for cornices."

"I thought you were a rag and bone man," I said. "I thought that's what you were shouting."

"Yes, well," said Errenbow. "Just shows you. Got any Edwardian basins with original taps? Authentic wooden bog-seats?"

"No. Did you see the garden chairs? With a lick of paint and . . ."

The hero-king gave a last derisory glance around, and blew his nose.

"It's just junk, this stuff," he said.

Sweet Smell of Excess

There are in this life few things more unsettling than not knowing what it is you smell of. One of the things that is more unsettling is not liking what it is you smell of, whatever it is, and probably the most unsettling thing of all is being unable to stop smelling of it, especially if it is borne in upon you that other people do not like it either.

I have just come up to my little room in Bar-sur-Loup to write this, and as I passed the *châtelaine* on the stairs, she flattened herself against the wall. Furthermore, there was a twistedness about her smile which told me, as little else could, that she shared common olfactory cause with the people in the establishment I had just left. For, despite the fact that Le Jarrerie is an open-air restaurant, the alfrescation was clearly of no help to a number of my fellow lunchers.

A man at the neighbouring table lowered his conk to his sizzling mullet in miserable suspicion; a young couple two whole tables away down-breeze drew towards each other, whispered, and craned around, sniffing like a couple of timorous okapi; and one elderly cove went so far as to stand up, walk to the edge of the terrace overlooking the Loup, and ostentatiously flare his nostrils at it for some considerable time.

I wondered whether to go through some such motion myself, in order to, as it were, throw them off the scent; but my wife reckoned this to be quite literally a bad move, since

30

as soon as the smell began to ambulate, it would invite differential coefficients which could spell even worse trouble. A moment's cross-plotting would enable the regulars to home in on me much in the manner of Gestapo scanners pin-pointing a suitcase transmitter.

Entering a mitigant plea of francophilia would not save me: "Who that truly loves France goes around mucking up lunch?" they would cry, as they bunged me into the foaming Loup, and the next thing I knew I would be bobbing off Antibes while yachted sheikhs excitedly emptied their Purdeys at me as a welcome break from the clay pigeons which normally seem to occupy their every seaborne moment.

Not that the French don't have themselves entirely to blame for my smell: their domestic electricity system is the most capriciously inconsistent in Europe. Hardly had Air France debouched us into Nice airport, kissed us on both cheeks and wished us a *bon séjour* in the hills behind, than I discovered the plug on my shaver to be a millimetre either too large or too small to fit into any of the holes our little hotel had to offer. There was thus nothing for it but to nip down the road to Vence and buy a safety razor.

At least, I thought there wasn't. It did not occur to me until the search took me past a gents' hairdresser that it might be fun to have what I have not had in twenty years: a professional shave. Especially as I had never had one in France, where a whole new world of invaluable idiom might be opened up to me – I should learn whether French midfield players went like trains and had educated left feet, I should be able to inform a stunned cab driver on the way back that the Marseilles lads played a blinder in the course of getting it together on the night and subsequently finding themselves over the moon.

In fact, it took me several minutes to explain that all I wanted was a shave. The barber wanted to give me a haircut. He did not like doing shaves without haircuts, mister had to understand it was only Fr20, compared with Fr50, but eventually we struck a deal on the basis that mister would

31

want hot towels (Fr10 extra), and mister sat down, whereupon the barber remained utterly silent throughout.

It was after he had boiled my face that he took the bottle out. He looked at it as one who has not looked at something for a long time. He up-ended it, and waited. Slowly, something fell into his palm. It was the colour of Pernod and it seemed to have the specific gravity of Bostik, and when he had a palmful of it, he kneaded it into my face.

Six hours have now passed, and I cannot get it off. It laughs at soap. I may smell of it until I die. Even then, I shall not know what it is called. What I do know is that there is a great perfume called *Je Reviens*, and that this is the opposite of it, so let us call it *Je Ne Reviens Pas*.

If only because that, I suspect, is what the barber was getting at.

Softly, a Word or Two Before You Go

Thirty years at the rockface and six million words chipped out, several of them different, but where is the slickness now, when all I need is a dozen or so? I suck the pencil-stub and stare at the wall, like a kindergartener paralysed by the orthographic options of "cat".

It is not my wall, it is Mr Jebb's wall. You can tell it is Mr Jebb's wall, because it has headstones leaning against it. They form the lugubrious backdrop to Mr Jebb, who is sitting on the other side of his desk, staring at me staring at the wall. The desk, like everything else here, has the faintest covering of white marble dust, the detritus of Mr Jebb's profession. The dust is the words Mr Jebb has himself chipped out over more working years than mine, and more literally, too. Mr Jebb is a stonemason.

We have convened on this bright morning, with yet more of Mr Jebb's old words turning and winking in the sunbeams as fortuitous metaphor of what we all end up as, in order to determine what to write on my father's gravestone. This itself would have tickled my old man no end: we went to a fair few funerals together, he and I, and we rarely walked away with a straight face. Death seemed always to tap an atypical subversiveness in him: he led – as far as I know – a straight and sober life, whose conventional virtues he appeared to take reasonably seriously, but only until that moment when some soapy graveside minister began extolling the late qualities of the snuffed. This was a moment at which you did not want to catch my old man's eye. And after it was all over, we would invariably take a stroll among the stones to speculate sacrilegiously upon what the words above were at pains not to say about the remains below.

What, now, shall I say of him? How do you sum a man up in a few chiselled syllables? How do you offer him a little originality to make the stroller pause? How do you express your own private regrets for public display?

"Personally," said Mr Jebb, after a bit, "I'd keep it simple. You cannot go far wrong with *Passed To His Eternal Rest Deeply Mourned By His Loving Family.*"

"It doesn't say much," I said.

"On the contrary," said Mr Jebb, "it says it all. I have done a lot of poetry in my time, I have done whole sonnets, you would not believe how many people want *Death be not proud* etcetera, 14 lines and you're praying you don't put the chisel wrong on the last one, and when you've finished it and you stand back, it's just another cliché, only longer."

"I was wondering whether something, er, lighthearted perhaps . . ."

"Another mistake," said Mr Jebb, firmly. "They don't wear well, jokes. You might just get away with – how shall I put it – a relevant pun, but personally I shouldn't advise it. I remember doing an old soldier, once, he left instructions requesting *A Better 'Ole*. It upset his family no end."

"I rather like it," I said. "I know my father would have done."

"He wasn't," inquired Mr Jebb, brightening, "a military man?"

"No. Well, he was in the RAF during the war, but . . ."

"Ah. You could have *Borne Up By The Eternal Wings*, then, or if it was Fleet Air Arm there's *Borne Away on the Eternal Deep*, usually naval, I admit, but you could stretch a point."

"It isn't him," I said, lamely.

Mr Jebb shrugged. "What was his profession?" he said.

"He was a builder."

"*He builded better than he knew/The conscious stone to beauty grew*," said Mr Jebb. "Ralph Waldo Emerson, and a personal favourite."

"I'm afraid he wasn't that kind of a builder," I said. "More of a decorator, really. You couldn't very well have *He plastered better than he knew*, could you?"

Mr Jebb sucked his lower lip. I shrugged.

"I suppose all I want to say, really," I said, "is that he was a nice bloke, and everybody misses him."

Mr Jebb shook his head. "It just wouldn't look right," he said, "once it was chiselled."

I put the pencil down. What suddenly mattered was that it wouldn't have mattered a damn to my old man.

"How about *Passed To His Eternal Rest Deeply Mourned By His Loving Family*?" I said.

"Very nice," said Mr Jebb. "Do you want a comma after *Rest*?"

Manifold Pressures

On Sunday afternoon I blipped the throttle, slipped the clutch, and set off for Delusion. It is a delightful part of the world, and though it is of course inexorably shrinking with every passing hour, you may still, on a good day, travel quite reasonable distances before hitting the frontier.

Sunday was just such a day. This greenhouse summer has been good to Sundays, and never more so than to those spent lolling in Delusion: it has been possible to drift in varnish-scented punts, and lie drowsing after boozy picnics, and wool-gather on the boundaries of middle-aged cricket matches, and float on one's back in Highgate Pond watching swallows hoover midges, and play tennis on hard lawns, and sluice down *al fresco* Pimm's far into the clement night – in short, to carry on not only as if there were no tomorrow, but as if there were still the yesterday of nostalgic fiction.

Especially if you had an open car. Even more especially, if you had bought it in April with the glum conviction that what you were actually forking out for was a cast-iron guarantee of a monsoon summer, to be spent aqua-planing down flooding motorways in search of a lay-by to bust your fingernails in as you fought to buckle a roof over glowering passengers with their coiffes plastered to their cheeks and cats and dogs rising up their shins.

In the event, not a bit of it: or, rather, not a drop of it. It has been a Dornford Yates summer, a summer recalling those cigarette cards on which every British car seemed to sail under canvas and which first programmed automotive romance into the susceptible tiny, as yet qualified only to shove battered Dinkies about. A summer when those of us who have *aficion* have been prepared to risk derision by not calling them convertibles any longer, but tourers, or ragtops, or even drophead coupés.

We have bought checked caps. The odd cravat has been sighted.

The only snag has been the backdrop for all this. The roads which posed for cigarette cards are thin on the ground, now. The stuff on which the open Frazer-Nashes and Lagondas stood, in yesteryear's pasteboard, would wind away behind them into the sunlit emptiness, between high hedgerows blazing with unsprayed flora: sometimes, there would be a rose-clad cottage, a tiny village shop, a yew-girt church, a smiling virgin in a dogcart, a smocked rustic tugging his forelock towards the shimmering cellulose of the gentry, a winsome cherub bowling a hoop past the for'ard bumper. They were pictures for blokes to stick under their tin hats when embarking for Normandy in order to remind themselves why they were going.

What you would put on a cigarette card now, God knows. A Nipponese Rover in front of a Little Chef, probably, with a coachload of Millwall supporters chucking contraflow cones at it.

Still, one drives in hope, and Sunday was a day that offered it. We had lunched splendidly with a mob of friends in a magical Oxfordshire garden, and, on leaving, decided to eschew the M40 in favour of the map's threadier veins. And, do you know, it all went rather well? Not only did all the villages which I had not seen in 30 years seem hardly to have changed, but there were actually poppies bobbing at the verges. Even the sporadic cornflower.

Could this idyll last? Would I be writing this if it had?

Approaching Aylesbury, the fuel-gauge light winked on. I knew there was a garage at the next cross-roads. At least, there had been, 30 years back, and why move a garage when

36

business could only have got better?

Nor was I wrong. It was still where it had been when I had last driven in, and they had filled the tank, checked the oil and water and tyres, free, and topped up the battery, free, and leathered the windscreen, free, and I was out in four minutes, because that is what garages did, then.

Last Sunday, I was out in 25. There were two dozen people before me in the queue. They were not, however, buying petrol. They were buying microwaved pizzas, horror videos, beachwear, cold drinks, hot drinks, electronic games, soft-porn magazines, baseball caps, digital watches, panatellas, personal stereo-sets, paperback books, cassettes, and molten Mars bars, because that is what garages do, now.

By the time I got back to the car, the sky had clouded. It wasn't raining, but I put the hood up anyway.

Now, Here's My Plan

Would a Freedom of Information Act make any difference? I ask myself. It is only one of a number of questions I ask myself on this broiling Tuesday morning, here at the elegant chipboard counter of the Central Area Planning Office of the London Borough of Barnet. It lies on the jostling list somewhere between *Why was Franz Kafka so generous towards bureaucracy?* and *Why didn't I bring a gun?*

A Freedom of Information Act would, I suspect, make no difference at all to the lady opposite.

"On no account are these plans to leave this office," she

says, for the second time. She touches these plans as she says it, with a mixture of tenderness and awe which persuades me that, if need be, she would throw herself across these plans. These plans would leave this office only under her dead body.

You could be forgiven for thinking that these were the plans of the Bruce-Partington submarine. You would be allowed the assumption that the Borough Surveyor had just mapped out the North-West Passage, or that the Borough Alchemist had hit upon a yet better method than the rates for manufacturing gold from nothing.

Even if these were merely plans to declare UDI for Barnet and cede regency to Pol Pot, their watchperson's unshiftability might be explicable. But they are none of these. They are the plans of my street. More than that, I have been personally invited by no less luminary a panjandrum than the Controller of Development Services to inspect them. But not only can I not borrow them, I cannot even copy them.

I have tried that: a Xerox machine hums tantalizingly behind the lady. "If I pay for the copying," I wheedle, "perhaps you . . ."

A look comes into her eyes which suggests that at any moment a foot might press a hidden buzzer to alert the Borough Minder.

"You are not permitted to remove these plans from this office," she mutters, "in any form."

You will possibly have guessed by now that these are not plans of my street as it is, they are plans of my street as it will be if a planning application gets its appalling way. They show my street with a school in it, and a school parking lot, and allweather-surface school playgrounds where there is currently grass. That grass is Cricklewood's sole green amenity.

As green amenities go, it may fall somewhat short of the Bois de Boulogne, but it also falls somewhat long of a private prep school for not only 300 small boys but 300 large mothers and the 300 even larger Volvo Estates which will, during each morning and evening rush-hour, decant the 300 small boys from a traffic jam likely to extend from my front gate to, at a conservative guess, just outside Leicester. When the notifications of this proposal arrived on our neighbourhood mats yesterday, the stunned communal silence was such that you could have heard the ash from Nicholas Ridley's fag drop.

That, however, is not a battle to be fought in these columns: at least, not yet. Today's more altruistic bleat is on behalf of all those of us who are about to be put upon, who are invited to exercise their entitlement to oppose the putting, but who are then stymied by incomprehensible regulations that make nonsense of the entitlement.

A neighbourhood meeting having been called, I have been delegated to collar the plans for mass scrutiny, not to say mass hysteria. But it cannot be done. The crackpot circumscription of our right to object means that I am allowed only to memorize them. Spies get a better deal: at least they can eat what they've memorized.

Under the custodian's beady eye, I set to, but it is impossible: there are plans not merely of the street, there are little sketches of this elevation and that, with proposed buildings on them and proposed cars and proposed little people walking about. If I try to remember where the cricket pavilion is going to be, I shall forget where the lavatories are; if I commit the groundsman's hut to memory, it will stay there only until I attempt to site the car park.

Mrs Thatcher errs. The French had the right idea about civil liberties. And if this evening I can persuade my neighbours to whip up a catchy anthem, fashion a few stout pikes, and march towards a Central Area Planning Office ripe for storming, I may yet persuade her that as far as Terror goes, sometimes there is no alternative.

Wild Card

American Express is up to something. This, of course, need not be an offence, even in the nimble-footed world of plastic credit: commercial enterprise requires that some things be regularly got up to, if heads are not merely to be kept above water but the noses on those heads kept in front of the field. Up must ever be the way with somethings, and, at mega-corporation level, they cannot be left – as you or I might leave them – simply to turn up: they have to be thought up, and dreamed up, and cooked up, by red-braced men in Perrier-filled rooms, who have convened in the hope of coming up with something which their company may then profitably get up to.

However, while getting up to something is unquestionably a way of describing the perfectly proper practices by which big business conducts itself, I should not choose so to describe them, did I not need also to suggest that there may, on occasion, be an iffiness in the air. A slight hum, a whiff. A hint that the something being got up to is not usually got up to without a nudge and a wink, nor even, perhaps, the slightest of smirks behind the hand.

American Express have written to me again. They do this quite often, because we go back a long way together, and it is one of the lessons of this life that those from whom we scrounge money tend to stay in touch. They do not always write to inquire about the money, of course, they sometimes write because they want to give me something – a few goblets, perhaps, a personal organizer, a ballpoint pen with a little calculator in the cap, asking no more of me than that I mention them to a friend or that I take out some insurance, or consider a cruise – the sort of topics chaps regularly bring up in their correspondence down the long arches of the years.

Until this week, though, they had never brought up the other thing chaps tend to bang on about. But this week, Mr Alan Stark, a Vice-President in Brighton (from none of which multiple resonances do I intend to make cheap capital) wrote: "Dear Mr Coren, what better way is there of turning a business trip into a pleasurable short break than having your partner come with you? Every year many thousands of American Express Cardmembers travel to France for both business and pleasure ... that is why I'm especially delighted to tell you about an exclusive offer – called *Take Your Partner* – negotiated on behalf of American Express Cardmembers with Air France. Quite simply, when you book your own Club Class ticket to France, buy a second ticket at the Excursion fare for your partner. Air France will then upgrade your partner's travel to Club, free of charge."

Fine. No problem there. Perfectly proper, and a smart deal too. Next time Coren & Partners, Purveyors of Light Hackwork Since 1961, nip over to Paris to see whether *Le Monde* is in the market for a gross or two of bilingual jests, I might very well take young Foskett of Punctuation with me. Get a lot of paperwork thrashed out on the plane, business lunch at Taillevent, then on to ...

But soft! What light through yonder brochure breaks? The little booklet Mr Stark has enclosed has a Parisian sunset on the cover, and strolling in this are two people. It is a Cardmember and his partner. The Cardmember – let us call him Mr Coren – has a businesslike briefcase in his hand, but it is not as businesslike as the arm he has around his partner. For the partner has a frock on. The partner is not young Foskett of Punctuation.

The partner is clearly not Mrs Coren, either, After all,

41

American Express know Mrs Coren well, they have carried on their own correspondence with her, they have addressed her personally; their computer-amanuensis could easily have invited Mr Coren to take Mrs Coren, but they carefully chose otherwise. They think Mr Coren might have what Channel-hoppers call *un petit peu à côté*.

They think that Mr Coren may himself be up to something.

I am not being prissy about this. These are liberated times. I want merely, as we're old buddies, to advise American Express of the shortcoming of their scheme. Because those who sidle off to Paris for naughties do not want their transactions recorded on the Amex computer. They prefer to pay cash.

It says less about them than a card ever can.

AUGUST

Where is my Island in the Sun?

"Can you see it, Dickie?" shouted Dickie's wife. We all waited. Fifty feet above us, up the steep slope of the garden, Dickie craned and peered. Above Dickie, in the pines, the *cigales* sawed away. Above the pines, the noonday Riviera sun gonged down.

"No," shouted Dickie eventually. The *cigales* stopped when Dickie shouted. They may have recognized that note in the voice which makes a man a leading actuary. Who can tell what impresses insects?

"I knew he wouldn't be able to see it," said Dickie's friend, Geoffrey. Geoffrey was happy that Dickie couldn't see it. Anyone could tell that from his voice.

Dickie slithered back down the slope to where the rest of us were sitting on the terrace, emptying bottles of this and that.

"I could see Antibes," said Dickie, a touch more breathless than he'd been when he left us five minutes before.

"We can all see Antibes," said Geoffrey's wife. "We can see Antibes from down here."

45

The six of us looked towards Antibes, 6km due south, rimming the Baie des Anges. It looked pretty good. It looked good enough for anybody, on this simmering day in the hills behind Vence: you looked down towards Antibes and the sharp blue of the Mediterranean, and you cooled by 10 degrees. This, however, wasn't enough for Dickie and Geoffrey. They wanted to see something else.

Or, rather, they didn't. They wanted to see something from the house they'd rented, but they didn't want to see it from our house, because they had paid a lot more to rent theirs, and the reason they had paid more was that they could see something from their house which they were now delighted to discover they couldn't see from ours.

They were 500ft higher up the mountain, and could see Corsica.

They hadn't seen it yet, though. They hadn't seen it because there had been haze on the sea for the week they had been here, and they couldn't see anything beyond rotten old Antibes. But then, this morning, le Mistral blew.

We woke to the noise of chairs flying low over the garden. The pines were bent double. The wind was barrelling up the valley of the Loup like a feral hobgoblin. When that happens, up here, men with wigs stay indoors. Big dogs get chained up. Small dogs get snatched inside, to stop them from being throttled as they sail to the ends of their tethers. People with cats just pray, and get ready to write poignant notes to pin on gateposts.

Then, just as suddenly, it stops, and the air is preternaturally clear. Razor edges appear on things which have hitherto been soft. And those whom estate agents have assured they will see Corsica might well see Corsica.

But Dickie and Geoffrey and their wives haven't, yet. They spent last night in Menton, and I met them in the Café du Midi in our village, where they had taken shelter from le Mistral on the way back to their very expensive house, because they didn't want anything to fall on their very expensive car, and rocks nip off cliffs during le Mistral. We got talking, and I suggested they drop in to us for a drink, and when the wind died, they did.

Where, after a while, you could tell they were growing restless.

"Look, let's drive up to our place for the other half," said Geoffrey.

"He wants to see Corsica," said Geoffrey's wife.

"I couldn't give a toss about Corsica," said Geoffrey.

"We bought a telescope in Menton," said Geoffrey's wife.

"We didn't buy it for that," said Geoffrey's friend, Dickie, quickly. "We don't need a telescope to see Corsica."

So we all drove up the hill, and theirs was unquestionably a very nice house, from the terrace of which you could see much more than you could from ours.

"Is that it, over there?" asked my wife, after a bit.

We gazed. The horizon was a steel rule. But, at one point, there seemed to be a slight deckle.

"I think it's a cloud," said Geoffrey's wife.

He looked at her for a moment.

"I'll get the telescope," said Dickie.

We all took it in turns to look through the telescope.

"You know what I think," said Geoffrey, when we had finished. "I think the bloody haze has come back."

"That would explain it," said Dickie.

On a Wing and a Prayer

Three o'clock in the morning, and one of them has got through.

One of them always will. That is the simultaneously

glorious and terrible truth about aerial bombardment. Whatever the quality of our defences – however vigilant our observers, however sophisticated our counter-measures, however devastating our protective ordnance, however many of the attackers plummet to oblivion through our unflinching ack-ack commitment – there will always be one flyer courageous enough, or foolhardy enough, or simply lucky enough, to push himself to limits unimagined by the tactical manuals and the aeroballistic boffins and the bunkered strategists; one who will, somehow, penetrate the impenetrable to press home the unpressable.

And all it takes, with a strike-weapon so deadly, is one.

I heard him before I saw him. You always do. Sometimes you never see him at all: you lurch awake to the tell-tale whine of battle-tuned engineering, you spring into evasive action, but it is already too late, the noise you heard was not the attacking dive but the post-operational climb – but, this time, I did. I heard him coming in high, and I grabbed the bedside torch, and I swept the blackouted dark, and suddenly there it was, caught in the searchlight beam, a tiny construct of dangling threads so preposterously frail that, despite myself, I could not help a stab of shock at the madness of sending a kid up in a crate like that.

It was of a design so crude you would have sworn it had gone out with the Ark, did you not know that the Ark was precisely what it had come in with. It had been smart on the Ark. For 40 days and 40 nights, it had stayed off Noah's neck, thereby avoiding that patriarchal swat which would have changed all our holidays. So here it was, above me now, coming in on a wing and a prayer.

Mosquito von Richthofen.

He gunned the throttle, banked into an Immelman turn, and plunged derisively out of the beam. As I swept the darkness I saw the rest of the squadron: dead to a gnat, their pitiful wrecks littering the bedroom floor.

What had got them that had not got him? Was it the deadly *No-Bite*, imported from Boots, a state-of-the-art SDI plug-in system no larger than a cricket-ball, yet "remove a

No-Bite tablet from foil and slide onto ceramic hotplate beneath the grid, insert the appliance plug into mains wall-socket, after one hour vapour emitted will then have cleared an average-sized double room of all flying insects?" If so, why was the Baron impervious?

How had he not been brought down by *Insecticide Kapo*? Bought locally from a ravishing pharmacist who, when I enquired as to its efficacy, indicated her own unblemished skin so fetchingly that sweat broke out on mine, *Insecticide Kapo's* label swore it would annihilate "*moustiques, mouches, punaises, pucerons, charançons, araignées, guêpes, taons, mites, puces, fourmis, cafards, blattes, et cancrelats*".

It showed corpses of things I had never seen, a dead *blatte*, perhaps, with its antennae crumpled, a riddled *guêpe*, a broken *taon*. Surely the item whining above me must have been one of these: what had it learned, back at Base, to render it immune to *Kapo*? We certainly weren't: I had sprayed the room before we turned in, and the stuff had the authority of Zyklon-B. It sand-papered your eyes: your tongue curled; you felt your hair falling out. Light a fag, and they would have heard the bang in Nice.

And then there was *Catch*. The stunning pharmacist had hardly wanted to sell me *Catch*. *Catch* was the ultimate deterrent; it could not be sold to under–16s. The list of things you shouldn't fire it near was twice as long as the list of things it killed. You could go on safari with *Catch* and come home with rhino.

At 3.30am I switched on the light, locked in on my darting target, and fired *Catch*. My wife, a heavy sleeper, woke, choked, and sprinted for the bathroom. Tears ran down my face. Slowly, the wardrobe door changed colour. But the quarry flew through it, like a Dambuster embracing tracer.

This morning, our bedroom reeks, still; yet I have a weal on my thigh like a puce marble. Somewhere out there, a mosquito is being debriefed, cheered to the echo, probably decorated. Today, he will rest up; and pray for, tonight, a hunter's moon.

Shelf Life

There is something extremely odd about the geography of supermarkets. I may not have studied it deeply, nor experienced it widely, nor even considered it generally: but I know one most peculiar aspect of it rather well, and I have experienced it in every one of the dozen or so countries in whose supermarkets I have stood, disorientated and uncertain, while the hurtling trolleys of oriented and certain foreigners have ricocheted off mine as their drivers glowered and babbled at the obstructive stranger that was within their gates.

The peculiar aspect is that whenever one is in a new and therefore uncharted supermarket, whether in Dundee or Stuttgart or Cairo, not knowing which way to turn for some simple staple, one invariably ends up in the pet food section. *Coren's Law states that after 20 minutes in any strange supermarket, anywhere in the world, a man looking for a loaf will always find himself being stared at by a shelf-length of cardboard cats.*

Sometimes cardboard dogs.

Occasionally cardboard canaries.

Quite why this should be so is a very great mystery indeed. A supermarket's is not a geography that has been arrived at by accident: Tesco and Leclerc and the A&P did not get where they are today by glacial flow or continental shift or volcanic lurch. The supermarketeers came to a large piece of world, bulldozed it flat, and then proceeded to refashion it

50

along strict lines (quite literally) laid down by experts versed in the ergonometry of shopping, to maximize profit.

In short, the experts put goods where people would want them to be. This had the further advantage of cost-saving on staff, since shoppers would not need to ask where anything was. In the ideal, the quintessential, the Platonic supermarket, the word loaf would come into the shopper's head, his hand would shoot out, and when it came back to his trolley, it would have a sliced brown wholemeal in it.

It would not have a tin of Moggynosh Kodchunks in it.

What, then, has caused this bizarre but universal flaw in the grand design? Pet food, after all, is likely to be the last item a stranger needs: Swedes do not fill their Volvos with budgies before popping off for their Torremolinos fortnight, you never see an Airedale sitting beside a Scottish couple flying off to visit the Taj Mahal, hamsters do not romp the Kitzbühel slopes around their tiny American owners – what glitch in the consummate canniness of the supermarketeers has allowed this profitless factor to establish itself, whereby a shopper keen to spend money on something he needs always ends up trapped amid the shelves of the only things he doesn't?

It is just possible that it is a mystery no longer. I have this noontime returned from the huge Leclerc in Vence, where it was, a mere hour ago, dawning upon me that this was neither flaw nor glitch at all: it was a trick of marketing strategy so brilliantly cunning as to administer the antidote simultaneously with the poison – irritation at the cunning by which one was being seduced was instantly mitigated by the recognition of the brilliance with which it had been done.

I had fetched up, after the statutory 20 minutes, staring at a display of (I swear) TV dinners for cats. The box explained that since this nourishing meal was odourless to humans, cats could be fed in living rooms alongside their loved ones; everyone could eat in front of *Voisins*. I laughed.

And, immediately, a French shopper beside me began talking about her cat, inquiring after mine, and so forth. And it suddenly struck me that this selfsame thing had

51

happened several times before, in other foreign supermarkets. Whereupon a codicil to *Coren's Law* sprang into my head: *pet-owners communicate with one another more quickly and more enthusiastically than any other sub-culture.* Within seconds, I had explained my shopping needs to this lady, within nano-seconds thereafter she had begun not only dragging me around the place but recommending all sorts of goodies, special deals, own-brand bargains and so forth, which I could never have sussed for myself. I thus ended up spending three times as much as I should have done unassisted.

For it is a truth universally acknowledged, that a single man in possession of a good fortune must be in want of a full trolley. And that is not my law, but the supermarketeer's.

One of our Bedrooms is Missing

I was floating in the pool, belly-up and uneasily aware that there was, after two weeks in France, rather more belly up than there had been at the start and that the reckoning on this careless gluttony would have to be settled with Ryvita and Perrier very soon if autumn was not to be spent pushing my gut around Cricklewood on a wheelbarrow, when, abruptly and utterly, the *cigales* stopped.

It meant someone was at the door. *Cigales* are reverse watch-dogs: they bang on incessantly until an untoward footfall sticks a toe in their territory, at which point 50 treefuls instantly clam up. I finned myself to the edge of the pool, and as I touched, sure enough, the doorbell in the house high above me clanged. The gut and I dragged ourselves out and wheezed up the 60 steep steps and padded through the shuttered premises, dripping on the tiling on which we should therefore skid on the way back, because we always do, and slid the catch, and the noonday glare flooded in, excoriating the eyeballs with white light, so that you half expected ET to scuttle in and head, squeaking ecstatically, for the shallow end.

But it wasn't ET. It was a Close Encounter for the Third Time. It was another lot. It was almost indistinguishable from the lot who rang the bell yesterday, who in their turn were exact replicas of the lot who rang it on Friday.

It consisted of a grinning English lad of about 20 with a peeled conk, a tattered T-shirt, and ancient jeans chewed off at the thigh; with, at his shoulder, the companion who in all probability chewed them off for him, one way or another – a tall foreign girl built mainly of legs and blue eyes who, when you look inquiringly at her, tosses her head so that a fan of fine blonde hair floats up from one brown shoulder and gently settles on the other. She does not speak; they never do. It is the boy who speaks. He always says the same thing.

"Is Giles here?"

"No," you always reply, "Giles is at home in London. He's coming out when we go back."

"Ah," the boy always then says, "only Giles said it would be okay to crash out here for a couple of days."

You say: "Are you a friend of Giles?"

He says: "Well, friend of a friend, sort of."

If these ritual exchanges sound to you like codes, if they have the *timbre* of passwords, you are not far wrong. France 1989 this might appear to be, but France 1943 is what it truly is: a country full of young Englishmen who have dropped out of the sky with no idea of where they are, with no money, with only the torn British uniforms they stand up in, sleeping rough, wandering lost, but clutching a scrap of paper upon which is scrawled the address of a safe house where – they have been assured – they will be sheltered, provendered, protected from authorities who strongly suspect them of being the saboteurs who aerosoled "Shed Boys Rul Frever" on the village war memorial, and, after a few recuperative days, sent on their plucky way with a fistful of local currency and directions on how to find the next mug.

They are all accompanied by long female Swedes they have somehow accumulated along the underground route, doubtless because neutrality by association is not be sneezed at when the chips are down and the *flics* suspect you of being a Millwall supporter or a lager rep.

Those who run the safe houses are English parents, not French communists. This is because French communists are smarter than they were 45 years ago: manifestos have been reworded in order to obviate the commitment to shell out to each according to his needs. French communists cannot be relied upon to say: "My refrigerator is your refrigerator, my wine rack is your wine rack."

So I looked at the kid, and I tried to persuade myself that he had just baled out of the rear turret of a riddled Lancaster, but it didn't quite work, this time; call it twice bitten, thrice shy if you will, and try to be sympathetic to a bloke who wishes to float his belly around a small pool without having to take constant evasive action against a tall blonde barrelling back and forth on her hundred lengths as laid down in her handbook, *How To Be A Swede*.

Cigales know a thing or two. When a stranger approaches, shutting up and lying doggo is the way to play it.

Plonkers

My host has a bob or two. More than that, and to his great credit, not to say great debit, he clearly enjoys chucking it about, and not merely on himself, either. Even more than that, he knows whereof he chucks: the holiday villa above Cap Ferrat to which he has invited us for lunch is a very beautiful eyrie indeed, the tasteful grandeur and incomparable outlook of which would, had he ever been fortunate enough to tie the bib on here, had sent Hitler scuttling back to Berchtesgaden in apoplectic envy. It has not one but two grass tennis courts, upon either of which Steve Davis would have no difficulty at all in knocking up a 147 break, and a swimming pool which might well, given the astonishing flora and the murmuring cascades tumbling down its secluding rocks, have been imported whole from Bali.

On and in these, the long-stay guests he has invited out from England to share his good fortune – and, as fortunes go, the odds are that there can be few better – are disporting themselves as his maid ushers us on to the terrace so that he can begin filling us with buck's fizz. Now, it is the quality of the orange juice which defines a good buck's fizz, and if the citrus is right it is impossible to guess the provenance of the bubbles. However, such is the splendour not only of the *mise-en-scène*, but also the nibbles which the maid is handing round – chunks of grilled lobster, *palourdes farcies*, crab claws – that when the host inquires after our opinion of his refreshment and invites a guess as to its component fizz, I reply, not really joking: "Oh, I don't know, Dom Perignon is it?"

His glee is unconfined. His grin dims the noonday sun. He slaps his thigh with such joyous vigour that sunburned guests wince and pucker.

"It's a tuppeny-halfpenny *cremant* from up the road!" he cries. "Twenty francs a bottle, to be exact – *and* a 5 per cent discount on the dozen!"

A good guest, I contrive, from my lounger, a *couchant* stagger, and an astonished gasp. But from the one beside me, another guest, a QC who has driven over from his own villa in a Mercedes convertible he keeps down here just for his holidays, snorts: "I pick it up for 17 in Grasse."

"It's a half-hour drive," says our host limply. There is no disguising the faint miff that has crept into his mien.

"Half the fun," says the QC.

And it dawned on me what the other half was.

It was a dawn which, when we sat down to lunch, bloomed to full morning. The first course was an astounding escalope of fresh foie gras: had Sydney Smith caught even one whiff of it, he would have fallen into a swoon from which he might never have bothered to recover, preferring instead to grasp heaven with both nostrils.

With it came the mandatory Sauterne.

I held it up. The colour was somewhat widdley, the nose just perceptible, the taste thin.

"It's a 15-franc job," said the QC. "Not bad at all."

"Try 12!" cried our host.

Much nodding followed this cry around the table. I nodded myself, though at what I wasn't absolutely certain. Here, after all, was a bloke who, back in his London club, would have offered me a tankard of 50-quid Château-d'Yquem to sluice down a blob of indifferent pâté without a second thought. And so it went on, throughout the subsequent and no less delicious courses: as the food went from strength to strength, the wine went from weakness to weakness, culminating in a St Sidoine from the Var, decanted into crystal pitchers for no other reason than that the 5-litre plastic tub in which it came would have defeated even the butler's sinewy wrist.

"This works out," said our host, lifting to the light a goblet with the colour and appeal of a bloodshot eye, "at 9 francs a bottle, would you believe?"

Well, yes, actually. All that is unbelievable is that, slice it how you will, wine-snobbery will ever raise its head, sniff, and ensure that the nose it sniffs with ends up being paid through.

Book Ends

It has come, as it must always come on the last day of the holidays, with the suitcases yawning and those desquamating scales of tan we had always planned to take home to England, but always knew we never should, drifting down on them like the first snowflakes of an early winter. What has come is the moment of half-truth.

Do we take the books back with us?

They are not what they were. They are read, now. And being read on holiday is very different from being read at home, where they remain clean and flat and all but indistinguishable from the state in which they left the bookseller's, crisp as a starched dickie. On holiday, they get read good and proper. They don't half go through it.

Here is Julian Barnes's *Before She Met Me*. It is swollen to twice its birth-size, a gross grey wadge of a thing, still reeking of the chlorine into which it plunged before being fished out and baked in the sun. Marinated and done to a turn, it will, if I carry it home again, sit on the shelf forever askew, silently recriminating. I shall not be able to look Julian in the eye again.

Here is *Fathers and Sons*, fortunate only in that Turgenev is no longer around to have my eye avoid his. I took it away to read again after 20 years, but I shan't be reading it a third time. Not all of it, anyhow: for whereas the Barnes has grown horribly fat, the Turgenev has grown horribly thin. Pages 132–144 are gone. I left it open one day when I went to lunch; it was a long lunch, which I took in the shade, but the book took in the gum-desiccating sun, and when I got back, pp 132–144 had, quite literally, flown. They are probably in Bordighera by now, infuriating some bibliophi-liac beachcomber.

But how can I throw it away?

It is a *book*, for God's sake!

And so is *The Russia House*. Though not, unhappily, exclusively. It is also an insecticide. It had the great misfortune to be the only hardback I took away with me, and it was therefore the weightiest object to hand on the bedside table when the thing came in. I did not know what the thing was then, nor do I know what the thing is now, except that it is considerably flatter than it was then. It was the size of a thumb, and black, and scuttled up the wall on far more legs than one would ever have thought necessary just for getting about the place; and since it was not a thing you would want to turn the light out on, I grabbed the le Carré without a second's thought and slammed it against the wall.

I shall carry the crunch with me to the grave. But shall I also carry le Carré? Cleverly, I had removed its dust-jacket soon after we arrived, so that it would not curl and crackle in the sun. The result of this is that I now have the ineradicable impress of a flattened thing on the front cover, caught forever in the instant of expiry, like those ghastly shadows left on Hiroshima walls. I feel queasy every time I look at it. Even if I put the spotless dust-jacket back, I shall know that the thing is still there, a micron more palpable than its ghost, which will probably follow me around forever, hag-riding my soul like some figment of Poe, unless I lay it here, leaving the book behind.

But not only is *The Russia House* a hardback, I haven't even read it, yet. I had been saving it up. I had not anticipated that the day would come when I wouldn't even be able to touch it. Is the price of squeamishness to be another £12.95 back in London, or do I wait for the paperback?

And as for jolly Jilly Cooper, *Rivals* is more full of tiny bugs of its own than a le Carré safehouse. Its 700 pages seem to have something midgey stuck to every margin. I blame my daughter, who, hooked inescapably on the fizzy plot, read straight through from cover to cover on one of those thundery Midi days when the air is thick with mites. Dare we bring it back to England? Even in death, these tiny remains might be giving off stuff which could change our entire ecological structure.

This, then, is the half-truth to whose moment I, standing here, have come: but why, in spite of all, do I really want to take these wrecks home? As soon as I find an answer I shall pack.

SEPTEMBER

Hooray for Cricklewood!

The millions of you with nothing better to think about will recall that exactly four weeks have passed since this rickety soapbox trembled beneath my fulminations (see p.37) anent the greenfield site opposite my house, and the ambitions of University College School to bung thereon a big brick swottery.

During those weeks I have been relaxing in France, putting the whole business out of my mind and jotting rough notes about my next book, a thriller in which a number of prominent people are horribly done to death in an equal number of extraordinarily inventive ways, with no apparent connection between them, until a brilliant young detective from Cricklewood CID suddenly twigs that they were all governors of University College School.

Home yesterday, I started to stroll across the road to see whether anything untoward . . . or, God forbid, toward . . . had been perpetrated in my absence. Structuralists among you will have observed that the stroll stopped. This was because a sign had gone up at the entrance to the greensward. I could not yet read it, and I stopped because I needed to prepare myself for the moment when I should be able to. What would it say? *Boys' Skyscraper Going Up, Another Fine Development by UCS Properties plc?*

I put the girded loin into gear, and walked on. The sign said: "Greystoke Productions Film Unit This Way."

After the colour had drained back into my cheeks, I peered past it to a ring of production pantechnicons, mobile canteens and sound-vans drawn into an encirclement much in the manner of covered wagons. Beyond these, and beneath a battery of cameras and lights, two teams of small boys were playing football.

Coo-er, was my first thought. My second was that during my absent month the fury of the Cricklewood communards had been such that UCS had chucked in the sponge and was now seeking to amortize its investment by leasing the site to film-makers. Film-makers, moreover, of a very serious order. For what could Greystoke Productions be but the company responsible for *Greystoke*, obviously reconvened for the purposes of *Greystoke II*, in which the subsequent career of Tarzan is charted; perhaps, who knows, to the climax in which he is summoned from Backbench-les-deux-Eglises to lead the Conservative Party?

Well, now. How were I and the other communards to react to this? A film industry was an altogether different kettle of development from a prep school. Giant wonky letters in the hillside spelling CRICKLEWOOD might upset some, but others might well feel the heart beat a mite faster at the prospect of Tinseltown. We might all get swimming pools and see Meryl Streep in the launderette. Hacks among us might be called in for emergency script-surgery at a tenner a word. To use of cat/child/lodger as extra, £5,000, used notes only. A series of *The Cricklewood Greats* could well see Barry Norman chirping on our very own front walls, a feature no estate agent could ignore in the imminent boom.

Of course, there would probably be a lot of wild parties, full of undraped nubilia trying to ingratiate itself with influential local journalists in the hope of a column-inch or two; but we should just have to learn to take the rough with the smooth.

Ambivalences jostling in my head, I walked down the path towards the bivouac. Much faded denim ambled among the snaking cables, but if there were major stars about, they evaded my discreet craning. Probably in make-up. Possibly snorting something behind the bike-shed. Having nervous breakdowns, perhaps. They do that.

Thus it was that, suddenly addressed, I jumped. A young man was inquiring whether he could help. He gave me his card. It said he was Jevon O'Neill.

No one called Jevon had ever come to Cricklewood before. I wanted to ask if he was any relation, because if you can call a girl Tatum, you might very well call a boy Jevon, but I didn't.

I merely said: "What's the film about?" He said: "It's a commercial for the *Sun*. We'll be gone by tea-time."

Their revels now are ended. The insubstantial pageant just went up the road in half a dozen trucks and took the baseless fabric of this vision with it. Jevon says the commercial goes out on ITV this Sunday, but I needn't worry. It doesn't mention Cricklewood.

End of the Rainbow

"**B**ut that's worth thinking about isn't it?" says the man in the blue waistcoat. He smiles again, his canines white and regular as a row of Rennies. "And by worth, we're not of course simply talking money

65

here. . ." He pauses, slips suavely from his nonchalant perch on the corner of the desk opposite me, strolls to the window, and glances out across the rolling downland. ". . . We're talking quality of life."

I have stood on the simmering Cricklewood pavement for half an hour, waiting for this man. I have brought him in under my roof, and this twaddle is what I get for my hospitality. I should like to stick one on the nose above the radiant bridgework, but I cannot. Not because this would offend the ancient Cricklewood obligation towards the stranger that is within thy gates, but because it would break my television set. For that is where the man is. The rolling downland should have alerted you to that. He is looking out of *his* window, not mine. His premises overlook sheep, not skips.

His sheep, in fact, want to sell me something, too. I know this because a telephone number has just materialized in front of them. They are Junksheep. He is Junkman.

What is he doing in my house?

Are you sitting uncomfortably? Then I'll begin.

So great is the alacrity with which each new medium of communication is corrupted for the purpose of off-loading tat that one could be forgiven for concluding that commerce was the sole begetter and purpose of language. In the beginning was the Word, and a split second after the beginning was the Junkword. The serpent slithers down the tree, raises its trilby as only serpents can, and smirks: "See this revolutionary new apple, modom? I am not asking three sins, I am not asking two sins, I am asking just one little peccadillo of the realm. It is tantamount to giving it away, just examine it for a bit in the comfort of your own tree and you will readily agree that . . ."

We have of course come a long way since then, to arrive at nowhere. Man's obsessive quest for ever better means of communicating with his fellows has gone far beyond the simple technology of lip and ear, and each time it has done so, trade has followed invention's flag. The postal system was developed to enable us to contact one another over longer distances, whereupon Junkmail was born. Man

66

installed the telephone, and the second time it rang, it was a Junkcall from Arthur Murray offering Man a fabulous introductory discount on six foxtrot lessons. Hardly had the newspaper become a voluntary habit than the Junkpaper became an involuntary one you could not kick, short of nailing up your letter-box. And a scant week after I had installed a fax machine and its £35 paper-roll, I made the mistake of taking my eye off it for long enough to allow an estate agent to pump several feet of unsolicited Junk ads on to my workfloor, at my expense.

I had thought that that was as irritating as Junklife could get, but I was of course wrong. Twice this month I have received uninvited Junkvideos. Or, rather, each time I received a terse *billet-doux* from the Post Office, informing me that a package was awaiting collection at Cricklewood Sorting Office. They could not be delivered because I was out when the postman called, and Junkvideos come swaddled in Jiffybags just large enough to be, er, unflappable. So he takes them back, and writes.

Naturally, you cannot bin his note. Who, advised that a parcel is pining for him, ignores the call? You thus tack yourself to the end of a broiling queue, and half an hour later the counterman calls to his invisible sidekick in the stacks, and eventually the sidekick comes back with your Jiffyjunk.

My first, last week, was a two-minute epic ambitious to sell me a car. My second, this week, starred sheep who wanted to flog me an annuity. Next week, there will be others, which I shall have to go and collect just in case they are not.

They are no use to me even as recyclable tape. What can you record in two minutes? Half a Ben Elton joke? One-fiftieth of *Casablanca*?

As to what the Cricklewood sorters think I'm getting, check their leer. "Another video, is it? I bet these cost a bob or two."

No doubt they do. But we're not talking money here. We're talking quality of life.

Making a Comeback

I n this business, you do not look gift horses in the mouth. You rip your shirt off and stick it on them. It is always, of course, something of a mug's punt, but if it does come off you can walk home whistling with 800 words jingling in your pocket. Which is why, last Tuesday, I went for Serendipity in the two o'clock at Camden Town.

I had spent a fraught morning ferreting among the somewhat louche ironmongeries of Camden Road in search of a device by which a postal cage could be attached to the back of a front door, and I should almost certainly be glazing your eyes with the account of that fruitless expedition now had my wanderings not eventually fetched me up at a forlorn spot labelled Rochester Square. A tumbledown island bordered by pre-war council flats, it would not have implored more than the passing tribute of an environmental sigh, if I had not caught a glimpse of a foundation stone on the mossy wall of a squat redbrick building in the middle.

I cannot resist foundation stones. Not only do they instantly call up poignant tableaux of dead mayors in top hats; they often baffle the imagination at the star they managed to pull to do the trowelling. Rochester Square did not disappoint. When I peered through the rusty railings, I read: *This foundation stone laid by Sir Arthur Conan Doyle.*

What could have coaxed, in 1926, the great man thither? A gumshoe seminary, perhaps, a violin factory, a cabmen's hostel? If I seemed to hear his ghost reiterate that it was a capital mistake to theorize before one had data, I might not have been mistaken: for, five yards further on, I came to a second inscription, this time beside the door: *Rochester Square Spiritual Temple*. And I suddenly recalled that Sir Arthur had indeed been much preoccupied with that bourne from which travellers were regularly nipping back.

Beneath the inscription hung a notice board. *Clairvoyance Every Tuesday 2pm*, it said, *Please Use Rear Entrance*. It was 1.55. I walked round the back, and through the open door into a little room curiously hung with old frocks. Here, some 20 elderly ladies were rummaging through piles of secondhand shoes. The rest of the room contained five rows of old bentwood chairs, unoccupied.

I sat down. After a moment, one of the ladies sat down beside me.

"God bless you," she said. She held up a pair of sandals. "I'm normally a 5," she said, "not a 6, but if you put a bit of felt in you'd never know these were 60p, would you?"

They all sat down after that, and another lady came round with a jar and we all put 40p in it, and the lady next to me said she hadn't seen me there before and was it because someone close had just entered the spirit plane, and I said not exactly, and she said that was all the better, if you tried to get in contact straight away you could be terribly disappointed, those transferring to the spirit plane had to have time to settle down, it was like moving to a new neighbourhood.

Mrs Denny, the medium, came in spot on two o'clock, a trim and cheerful lady in a brown twin-set, and was immediately asked whether she had found her cat. She said yes, it had come back last Friday, but in the afternoon her other cat had been run over. At this, there was a general exhalation of sympathy, but Mrs Denny didn't seem too downcast, doubtless because cats translate to the spirit plane, too, and instead launched briskly into a flurry of messages, going along the rows in strict succession.

A number of husbands came through, occasionally identified by name, and in one case by the size of his head (small), and then Mrs Denny looked at me. There was a long pause. I felt rather odd. I have a lot of dead friends and relatives, and I couldn't help suspending enough disbelief to imagine them pushing and shoving to get to that point on the spirit plane where they could bend Mrs Denny's ear.

But nobody came. All that Mrs Denny said was: "Don't worry about your financial problems, your spirit friends tell me they will help."

A number of heads turned to gaze at me, sympathetically. I wondered if I looked like a man whose money had just died.

Not that I have any financial problems, as far as I know. What I don't know, of course, is how far that is.

Are There Any More at Home Like You?

Y ou will never know how desperately I wanted to write "Gun crew of *HMS Ambiguous* in spare room, list of names follows under separate cover, also disfigured opera-buff in cellar, identity unknown," in the space provided, but, however long I sat chewing my pen, I finally dared not. A man with a briefcase would have come round. Possibly accompanied by a dog-handler.

I do not know the penalties which attach to a false Electoral Roll declaration, but they are doubtless severe. A householder could well find himself in a highly embarrassing situation: it cannot be easy for a new bug to stand in the slopping-out line at Parkhurst and sheepishly admit to inquisitive axe murderers that he is doing three years for the inability to resist a question concerning the number of serving sailors and lodgers on his premises.

So, last Sunday morning, I merely entered the family names, licked the flap, and cursing myself for my weediness, bunged the thing off. It was only when I returned from the pillar box and opened the newspaper I had collected on the way back that I swore by the power I had just vested in myself that I should never again vote for Margaret Thatcher.

I do not know if there is a clinical designation of the disorder from which I have always suffered. It may appear in the textbooks as a mild form of Tourette's Syndrome, that unfortunate sociopathic quirk which drives its hapless victims to shout swear words in public places for no better reason than that they cannot help themselves, or it may be possible to look it up under Munchausen's Disease, where similar helplessness attaches to the compulsive telling of whoppers, since the complaint draws freely on the characteristics of both. It is, in short, an overwhelming urge, when offered any kind of form, to fill it with gross and elaborate lies calculated to unsettle the recipient.

Well, almost overwhelming. A sort of canny gutlessness stops me just short of doing it on forms where threats append: while I have to fight the longing to enter *terrorist* on visa applications, or *blind* on motor insurance proposals, or *£53,000,000 and counting* on tax returns, it is invariably fought successfully. But when it can be got away with – a buttonholing High Street clipboard, a junk-mailed application form for a credit card I do not want, a loose magazine insert probing consumer habits – a wave of mischievous fantasy wells up which brooks no damming. I can scribble for hours.

But the dream, of course, the fondest hope, the most fervent prayer of the true Munchette sufferer is to find himself staring at an important, official, above all *Government* questionnaire, on which no threat against mendacity, however couched, however stern, could ever be enforced. For no one will come to your front door and say: "This bit about wearing cricket pads and a *pickelhauber* while nude mulatto milkmaids throw doughnuts at you, all true is it?"

71

Thatcher Vetoes National Sex Survey is thus the most infuriating headline ever set in type. For my own informal researches persuade me that I am far from alone in feeling that itch in the pencil which comes on at the sight of a tickable box. What yarns we could have spun, you and I, what diagrams we could have drawn, what statistics we could have invented! What a stunningly comprehensive picture, above all, would finally have emerged of our national imagination! We should of course have derived no more inkling than we have now of what the British get up to, but, by heavens, we should have been offered a corking insight into what they don't.

The woman is quite mad. Were there ever more preposterous grounds for any political decision than her stated conviction that people would consider the survey an invasion of privacy? It is, after all, highly unlikely that any citizen would have been manacled to a desk and forced to spill his most intimate beans by stern Home Office disciplinarians – unless of course he had so stated this preference in the box provided.

The only probable backlash is the political one. For what could more effectively endorse the gibe that ours has become a nanny society than this monitory shriek from the Downing Street kindergarten enjoining us always to keep a hold of Nurse for fear of finding something worse?

Bloomers

Graham Greene scripted Tuesday for me, and Hitch-cock directed it. I merely stumbled wonkily through it, a couple of microns less sleek than Cary Grant perhaps, a pound or two unwirier than James Stewart possibly, but no less flummoxed than either.

Greenecock Productions began it, true to form, with a flashback to last Friday in, of course, The Polish Club in Prince's Gate. I shall not linger on this hitherto unvisited location, since I shall have more to say about it next week after Ms Kaczmarowska has painted my portrait – always provided that the purring invitation to her Kensington atelier does not, tomorrow, turn out to be a lure dangled on behalf of the Baltic Brotherhood, who plan, inexplicably, to whisk me to some gelid basement and plug electrodes into my temples – but for now, let me just say that last Friday midnight, a Pole I do not know came up to me and urged me to visit an exhibition entitled *A Tale of Two Cities* at the Royal Horticultural Hall, Vincent Square.

Curious as this was, I thought no more about it until Tuesday (vodka can do that to you), when a loose end put itself up for grabs. I drove to Vincent Square. I could not see the Royal Horticultural Hall, but beyond the railings beside my parking-meter, a groundsman was sitting on the bound-ary of the cricket pitch servicing a motor-roller for hiberna-tion, so I approached, and was about to inquire, when he said:

"Looking for the Royal Horticultural Hall?"
As it were "*Looking for the 39 steps?*"
"As a matter of fact, yes," I replied.

He pointed, mutely, and bent once more to his carburettor.

I paced out his fingerline down Greycoat Street to a large, but oddly unlabelled building. Nor was there a poster to flag its exhibition; only a blackboard stood outside, the scrawled chalk on which read:

Accountancy tutors: 1st and 2nd Floor. Toilets: Ladies, 2nd Floor, Gents, 3rd Floor.

I walked into the foyer, and joined a queue of anoraks shuffling towards the guichet. The man in front of me said: "Have you tried riding Rene?" The one beside him replied: "No. I'm a Talbot Bolero man."

The brain floundered. I know something of cars, but I had never heard of the Talbot Bolero. And what was Rene? A grey mare? A pet-named motor-bike? Some other old banger? They took their tickets, and I put my £1.50 on the counter, and followed them up the grey marble steps, into the enormous hall.

There were, at a rough estimate, between two and three million chrysanthemums in it. They were the biggest chrysanthemums I had ever seen.

"This is never *A Tale of Two Cities*," I said to the man on the door.

"That's in the Old Hall," he said. "This is the New Hall. This is the National Chrysanthemum Society Show."

It was also Greeneland.

Through the serried ranks of overblown cultivars and their dense dank exhalation, silent bloom-buffs moved, nodding, jotting, and, when they caught my eye, looking quickly away.

I had stumbled into The Ministry of Fear. Any moment, I should be asked to guess the weight of Elsie King.

Or Tracy Waller, or Marion Gosling, or Doreen Hall or Marlene Jones; for this is what chrysanthemums, it seems, are called. When they are not, that is, called Riding Rene or

Talbot Bolero. I had entered a world of eerie and impenetrable codes. What is a floritect bloomguard? What is a birky bag? What is pennine jade? On a dais at the rear, two men sat guard beneath a sign which read: *Plants To Which The Committees Were Unable To Recommend Any Award.* Beside them, the shamed pariahs wilted in their vases.

But I had paid my thirty bob, and I stayed the course. At the exit, a man offered me a Jakes Bag. "Elizabethans used them to sweeten the air in their privies," he explained. I should have taken it. Not that I have an unsweet privy, but because his was the only attempt at contact, and I might have learned why I had been sent.

Sent?

As I was unlocking my car, I noticed that the groundsman, on the further boundary now, was talking to the man from The Polish Club.

Sitting Target

With one bound, I was free (*vide* Chapter 1: *Bloomers*). The man from The Polish Club who was talking to the Vincent Square groundsman turns out actually to live in Vincent Square, and apparently recommends Royal Horticultural Hall exhibitions to everybody.

The National Chrysanthemum Society is not a KGB front organization. The Polish Club is not an assassination bureau. Elsie King has massive but well-formed spherical

75

blooms, faintly pink at the centre, though not as pronounced as its parent, World of Sport, and is, I am informed, aptly named after a larger-than-life personality with a warm heart. A Floritect Bloomguard is a patent cage which cossets cultivars travelling by Volvo.

I am indebted to the many well-wishers who have written to me to put this labyrinthine record straight. Also to one ill-wisher.

Furthermore, la Kaczmarowska turns out to be not a slinky seductress masquerading as a brilliant portrait artist, but a brilliant portrait artist masquerading as a slinky seductress. True, as the result of her insinuation into my life, I shall end up hanging in The Polish Club, but only – contrary to last week's fears – in effigy. Pastel, to be precise.

I knew she wasn't a slinky seductress the moment she opened her studio door to my timorous tap.

"Good afternoon, Miss Kaczmarowska," I said.

"Call me Basher," she replied.

This was not, as far as I know, an invitation ever extended by Marlene Dietrich: certainly, it was a far cry from "*It took more than one man to change my name to Shanghai Lil.*" Whether this was a source of relief or disappointment to me, however, I have given up pondering.

New readers may wish to know – a long shot, I grant you – that Basher and I met on the Friday before last at The Polish Club, whither we had been beckoned by our mutual friend, Sir Clive Sinclair, to help him and a gross or two of tuxedoéd guests see off a lot of vodka and *charcuterie*.

By midnight (as the result, I am convinced, of their having put something in the salami) the room seemed to have become rhomboid, but I was managing to negotiate it relatively well, so that, just after I had been button-holed by the Pole from Vincent Square and was carefully making my way down the 1-in-4 Axminster again, I was able to fetch up against the lovely Ms Kaczmarowska quite gently, ie, without spilling anything out of either my glass or her dress, and very soon thereafter, she was generously offering to chalk my face.

As I had never been to Stanhope Gardens, I accepted, Mysterious blondes, as you would expect, thread through my daily life like Fair Isle woof, but opportunities to visit SW7 are scant.

Basher (possibly, on reflection, Basha, or even, given the orthographic plenitude of her race, Bacszscza) proved to be every bit as good as her throaty word. Basher was, quite literally, a dab hand.

The studio was hung with her wondrous dabbings of the great, the good, and, it must be said, the seriously loaded. Were she able to translate my elusive essence to cartridge paper, then I, too, should have a hat-peg in that august pantheon whose doings keep the wolf from Nigel Dempster's manhole cover.

But what *was* that essence? Hardly had Basher flung me into a wicker chair and herself at her easel, than trouble brewed. It lay in the smile. My entire personality, in her judgement, resided in a couple of millimetres of lip. But only sometimes, and, to me, unwittingly.

It is not easy to sit motionless for three hours trying to summon up a quizzical curl for somebody else, and, having struck what they want, thereafter prevent it from freezing into a shifty smirk.

Sitting at all is nightmare enough, with an artist's eye gimletting your core, but having to do it in the knowledge that everything you are is apparently contained in one fleeting expression which you yourself are unable to envisage *in situ* is inexpressibly unsettling.

Though not half as unsettling as examining, at last, the result, finding it exactly as you think yourself to be, and being told by the person who has done it that it is not.

For how will you ever know which of you is right?

OCTOBER

Death in the Afternoon

In Cricklewood, last Saturday, you could not eat, drink or smoke. September 30 is a ritual day.

It is perhaps the biggest ritual day in the Cricklewood calendar. It is so big that it involves not only fasting and prayer, but also a unique method of breathing. You have to breathe in quick shallow gasps, eschewing the deep inhalations and leisurely expulsions of the days which are not September 30. That is because the air is thick with pungent incense. And since the incense is compounded of ureic nitrogen and dichlorprop and sulphate of ammonia, you do not want to invite it to hang around the lung.

You have not, after all, got pearlwort on the lung.

For September 30 is Weedkiller Day. It is the last day on which lawns may be treated. It says so on the bottles of weedicidal gunge which for many months past we have been keeping away from pets and children.

The label told us we could have applied it from April to September, but we heeded it not, and September 30 is thus the day when the sins of omission come home to roost.

And severe indeed are the penalties for leaving undone

those things which we ought to have done, and having done those things which we ought not to have done. Because for lolling on lawns with a mixture of 5 parts gin to one part dry vermouth, when we should have been trudging back and forth across them with a mixture of 500 parts water to one part weedkiller, a high price must finally be exacted.

The day begins with a reading from the text. You take the bottle from its pet-proof shelf, and you observe that it will kill buttercups, clover, daisy, dandelion, dock, hawkbit, knapweed, pearlwort, plantains, mouse-ear chickweed, sorrels and something imponderably called selfheal. Good: you have looked at the lawn, and it seems to have all that – whatever it is – sprouting out of it. Indeed, it has got everything on it except grass.

It is when you reach paragraph two that unease begins to churn: "The following may require different treatment – yarrow, speedwell, yellow suckling clover, field woodrush . . ."

You now go out and peer more closely. Is that mere hawkbit, or could it be yarrow? Is that common clover or yellow suckling clover? Crouched close to it, you observe it to be quite yellow, really, but is that simply because, this being September 30, it has fallen into the sere, or is it actually suckling something?

The penitence begins. Because you wish to produce something more for your hours of back-breaking pesticide than an immune vegetable sneer, there is nothing for it but to snatch up representative handfuls of weed, hurtle to the garden centre, and join a long queue of other people clutching similar bunches, like so many infants waiting to press posies upon some wing-inaugurating nabob, until the man at the till can peer at the wilted detritus in your fist and explain that your passage to the safe side will be £23.19.

It is noon by the time you bring the new bottles back, and you know the rest of the queue has arrived before you because the whole of Cricklewood now smells like Scutari. It is amazing that dead cats are not falling off every fence. This is the point at which you read the new labels and discover that the stuff is not to be applied during a drought. As there has been a drought since about February, you must now water the lawn.

This brings you to 4 pm, and the moment when the first measures of mixed gunk may be introduced to the first of a hundred canfuls of water, so that the first 5 sq yds may be sprinkled. You know what 5 sq yds looks like, because you have measured them, and it is still light.

By 6 pm, however, the gloaming is afoot: sometimes you do 3 sq yds, sometimes 10. You would like a cup of tea and a fag, but you cannot, because you have been dispensing gunk, and if you touch your lip, it will fall off tomorrow.

And tomorrow is looming. By 8 pm, you are lurching through the blackness and firing at will, praying that what you are hitting is a sq yd and not a pet. From the enticing glow of a distant room, the guests who have turned up for dinner are peering out, but you cannot join them. Not for you the loud bassoon.

Out here in the darkness, you are racing field woodrush to the tape.

Business in Deep Waters

It all began in East Ham, last Monday, and it will all end off Brighton, though when I do not know. But I can wait.

The obsequies for my 97-year-old step-grandmother having drawn to their close, I was walking back through the cemetery when a mourner beside me said: "She booked the plot years ago." He paused. "Course, it was all green fields, then."

Who could not take his discreetly covert point? Time, like an ever-rolling concrete mixer, had left the little graveyard an island entirely surrounded by exhaust distributors, DIY supermarkets, kebab dispensaries, video factors, cut-price carpetmongers, and suchlike cultural boons.

The cemetery was just another High Street facility. It was probably time to describe it as a soul outlet. It was not, in short, a place you'd want to be caught dead in.

This reflection dogged me as I drove home through the bleak streets. I had never hitherto given any thought whatever to my posthumous disposal. I have enough on my plate without filling in a lot of forms specifying brass handles and fugues, never mind quartering the map in search of a suitable knoll and yew. Now, though, I began to think about it; and as I did, I realized I did not wish to be interred next to a multi-storey car park, or indeed, if future Lady Porters had their way, under it. Which latter, of course, lay at the nub: the pastoral tract you book today could well have space shuttles landing on it tomorrow. Next morning, I heaved open the Yellow Pages at *Funeral Directors*, and dialled Nodes, selected for no better reason than the name's fine Dickensian ring. They would know where to lay their hands on plumes.

No problem, said Nodes, Hampstead cemetery was at the top of my road, there was still bags of space, and if I didn't hang about too long I could very well find myself under a nice tree.

I considered this. I know Hampstead cemetery well; it is my short cut to the Nautilus Fish Bar. I have seen people throw unwanted hake over the railings before now, and the dogs never read the Keep Out signs.

I asked Nodes for options, and they said Hoop Lane would be only too glad to cremate me, but I said that I had never fancied that, and, after a little more funeral chat, what can only be described as a note of polite exhaustion came into the Nodes voice as it said: "Have you thought of being buried at sea?"

"Scattered, you mean? I'd have to be cremated first."

"Not so. Permission for sea-burial may be obtained from most harbourmasters."

I hung up, stunned. Sea burial would be just the ticket. They couldn't put a block of flats up on the rolling deep. Even if a dog swam that far out, it certainly wouldn't swim that far down.

All I needed to do was choose my spot of main. It did not take long: I have always liked Brighton – very bracing. Of scant use to me, perhaps, but the mourners could get a breath of fresh air and a plate of fresh winkles, and the day would thus not be entirely wasted.

So I rang the Shoreham Harbourmaster. I would, he explained, need to get a licence from the Ministry of Agriculture, Fisheries and Food. A bit unsettling those last two responsibilities, but I rang anyway.

"No problem," said an extremely nice Agfish man. "It does come under The Dumping At Sea Act 1974, I'm afraid, now incorporated in The Food and Environment Act 1985, but don't let that put you off. If I may say so, you couldn't have chosen a more ecologically sound course. Ring 238 5872, and Mrs Pullinger will give you the details."

Mrs Pullinger was charm itself.

"Several areas off the South Coast are suitable," she said, "but we do obviously prefer the deceased to be in a shroud rather than a coffin."

"I quite understand," I said, albeit faintly.

"If you insisted on a coffin," she said gently, "it would have to be weighted down and have holes drilled in it. The weights," she added, "must be of a material that would not harm fish."

"Of course," I said.

So that's it. Upon my decease, my loved ones merely contact Mr Whyatt at the Fisheries Office, Breeds Place (sic), Hastings, who will take it from there, even as I am taken from here.

Be nice to make a bit of a splash.

'Tis the Voice of the Lobster

When I say that I do not know what the French is for *fatherhood*, I do not mean I cannot lick the thumb as well as the next man and flick through Cassell's until it coughs up *paternité*.

What I mean is that I do not know whether *paternité* carries the resonances struck by *fatherhood*. Does it merely describe the state, or does it also adumbrate the role? Does it cover the quality of being a father as well as the quantity? Has it, in short, got fatherhoodness in it?

I do not, of course, need to know what it's called in order to recognize it when I see it; but having seen it, last Thursday evening, and thought about it several times since, I have been wondering what popped into the heads of all the French observers who saw it when *fatherhood* popped into mine. Especially as what I saw seemed to me to be an essentially Gallic example. However, let us dump fruitless semantic speculation, and address ourselves *à nos moutons*.

Or, rather, *à notre soupe de poissons*, this being the item simmering beneath the nostril on the night in question and, indeed, one of the main reasons the nostril had flown to Nice earlier.

Every few weeks, the craving comes for a three-day Riviera hog, and since BA343 whisks one door-to-*porte* in less than four hours, why, we have always cried as the knife rattles in the piggy bank slot, spend twice as much on one of those English gourmet weekends which inadequately fabricate the authentic? Especially given the decor in which they do it: while I yield to no one in my admiration for Colefax and Fowler, they cannot hold a candle to Alps and Mediterranean.

Thus, there I was in Nounou, fish restaurant nonpareil, corner table overlooking Golfe Juan, orange moon overlooking me, and anticipative nostril overlooking the *soupe de poissons*. It is a joyous dish, not least because you can play with it: it evokes the days when you dug ravines in porridge mountains and sent warm syrup rivers coursing through them. You launch the toast discs in the soup, pile the *rouille* aboard, sprinkle the grated cheese thereon, and eat the ones that capsize first. (Don't look up *rouille* in Cassell's, it offers only *rust, mildew* or *blight*, God knows why. Probably Cassell didn't get out much, had a Marmite sandwich on his desk, who can say?)

Anyway, I was happily splashing about in my dinner when I noticed a lobster come up at ear-height. It hovered over the next table, waving and having a last look around the way they do, and having got the approbatory nod from the plump diner beneath, it was borne off to the kitchen.

The plump diner was not alone. With him were his wife, a teenage daughter, her younger sister and, youngest of all, a little boy of perhaps four. It was even as my wife and I were murmuring – the way the English invariably do – about the charm, manners, turnout and, above all, sophistication of French tinies at the nocturnal table, that the boy began first to sniff, then to weep. His mother reached towards him, but he turned sharply away, muttering between sobs; whereupon his father leaned down, ear to the trembling lip, and, having listened, pushed his chair back and marched briskly out.

Readers who can smell happy endings a mile off will know what happened next. After perhaps a minute, the lobster came back, not this time in the waiter's grasp, but in the father's. What was going through the lobster's mind at this point is not easy to guess, but if it was occupying itself with the unpredictability of biped behaviour, it was not far

87

wrong. The father's other, unlobstered, hand now took hold of the little boy's and, Nounou's doors giving out directly on to a shingle beach, the three of them proceeded outside, crunched along the strand to, a few yards off, a little jetty and, having walked to the end of it, launched the father's erstwhile entrée into the sea.

I had half expected that when the pair came back into the restaurant the other diners would applaud; that they didn't may be attributable either to the fact that many of them were sitting in front of plates piled with embarrassing dismemberment, or that the shock of watching a man send 200 francs swimming towards Africa had irremediably compromised their approval.

Or, in one case at least, that they were too busy wondering how, in similar circumstances, their own fatherhood would have shaped up.

Driving Past

It is just as well that I am too old for trench warfare. I could not go over the top with a wallet like mine.

You know the scene. The Next Lot has broken out, self-preservation has dictated a nuclear stand-off, a conventional stalemate has duly been reached, and the Queen's Own Cricklewood Borderers are dug in around the shattered remnants of Wipers New Town, creeping into No-man's Land only to snip holes in the enemy wire, loot chicken nuggets from a rubbled McDonald's, or collect images for ironic sonnets.

It is on one such mad but unutterably brave foray that I – they call me Uncle, by the way, which compels me to volunteer for everything – am caught in the Very flare, and comprehensively enfiladed. All sorts of bits fly off me, and, despite carrying a thick family bible in every pocket, I fall, riddled, into a shell crater.

Someone is already in it. Let us – for I should not be there had things not gone so badly wrong that Gorby was forced to raise the Narodny base rate to 15 per cent and been ousted by the Old Guard, who have returned to the Old Ways – call him Ivan. He is rather like me: just an ordinary bloke, full of big holes. And it is pitifully clear that just as I shall never see Cricklewood Broadway again, he will never see Nevski Prospekt.

It is at this point – since neither of us is a stranger to the cinema – that he gropes in his blood-sodden battledress and eventually produces his wallet. He flips it open. There is a creased photograph of a careworn but still comely woman with her slim arms around three smiling children. I nod; but I do not respond. He, however, with a terrible effort, reaches out and taps my breast-pocket. There is nothing for it but to extract my own wallet with my one good hand, and open it. A creased photograph is revealed. It is of a scarlet 1963 Austin-Healey 3000, in pristine nick, never had a spanner on her.

It is a tricky moment. Not only does Ivan's photograph remind him of what he is fighting for, my photograph reminds him of what he is fighting against. Never mind *mon semblable, mon frère*, with his last breath he sticks his bayonet in me.

I retail this scenario which has long haunted me only because, without it, you will not be able to understand the unsettling coda which became attached to it last Sunday, and I know how much you want to do that.

Quite why that snapshot is the only one in my wallet, I am not entirely certain, but nevertheless I have been carrying it ever since August 1969, when I drove the car to Queen Charlotte's Hospital to collect my wife and first-born, and found that the carry-cot containing my first-born would not fit into it. The Healey had a tiny space behind its front seats, true, but the only way this would accommodate a carry-cot was with the roof down, and the last thing we wanted was to have the wind pluck out our first-born as we were belting round Hyde Park Corner. So we drove home with the infant lolling in its mother's lap, and the next day I traded the Healey in for a four-seater. Call it a rite of passage.

For some time thereafter I would occasionally take out its picture and gaze at it, especially if I bumped into somebody who drove one and looked as though he needed boring for an hour or two, but eventually, around, I suppose, 1980, it became permanently enpocketed among a detritus of old visiting cards and receipts and emergency Elastoplasts, and I never looked at it again. Indeed, I stopped thinking about the car itself; beginning to rust even as I sold it ("See that?" cried the dealer, "Poke your finger under there, they're buggers for corrosion, these"), it had, surely, long since gone down the road to Nineveh and Tyre.

Last Sunday, it passed me on the North Circular. It was going like a cliché out of hell, yet not so fast that I could not read 167 HOO on the number-plate. But when I tell you that I did not accelerate to catch it, do not assume that I did not care to meet the flashy swine who was fondling my steering-wheel, nor that I dared not discover how well it might be flourishing under his cuckolding care.

Good God, it's only a car. You can see that in the photograph.

When Push Comes to Shove

Be still, my beating heart! There is not long to wait, nor far to journey. October 27 is nearly here, and Clitterhouse Playing Fields but a short step down the Cricklewood byways.

October 27 is a big day in the history of Clitterhouse Playing Fields. Could be the biggest. It is the day of the Mobile Bin Exhibition. It is the day when the burghers of Cricklewood, having wound their way to Clitterhouse Playing Fields, will be shown not only their new mobile dustbins, but how to take best advantage of that mobility. Mr A.G. Williams, Director of Technical Services to the London Borough of Barnet (*aka* the Fiefdom of Cricklewood Without), is sending a crack team to show us how to push our new mobile bins up and down, do the thing with the lid, all that. Friday, October 27, is thus nearly as big a day as Monday, December 11. For Monday, December 11, is the day the bins go into service. Monday, December 11, is a red litter day.

All this I know, because Mr A. G. Williams has just sent me his bin brochure. It is a pretty zappy number, to the clearly expensive production of which no ratepayer could possibly take exception: fashionably green, glossy, smartly printed and laid out, its cover sporting a charming photograph of a lady ecstatically wheeling her new bin about, the brochure does the borough proud. A ratepayer could hold his head up anywhere, with a brochure like that in his fist. If

Lorenzo de' Medici had wanted to change the garbage system of Florence, Michelangelo himself could not have done him a better brochure.

It begins "Dear Householder", in engagingly fabricated longhand, but immediately goes into typeface for the serious business in hand. This starts with a concise history of Barnet rubbish since 1964, taking in the astonishing diversification of detritus, the rise of the plastic bag, the proliferation of supermarket cardboard, and how the galloping consumption of the average household has come to spell curtains for what it calls the traditional dustbin. There is also a trenchant little sentence about windy weather and the risk to binmen running about in pursuit of things blowing past them.

Thus softened up, we reach the nub: "*A wheeled bin/front gate system of collection will be introduced throughout the borough on Monday, 11th December 1989.*"

Semanticists will feel the neck-hairs rise. A wheeled bin/front gate system of collection is not a system of collection, it is a system of pushing a wheeled bin to the front gate. We know this will not be done by a collector, because the people who will be doing it are going to be shown how to do it at Clitterhouse Playing Fields on October 27.

But let that pass. Since I already clear the street outside my house of jetsam because the council doesn't, and prune the trees because the council doesn't, and prise the weeds from the bitumen verge because the council doesn't, and also do my – literally – level best to flatten the paving-slabs out, because the council doesn't, I have long come to regard rates as a contribution to charity, and if I can save a council dustman from running after storm-toss'd rubbish by the simple expedient of doing it myself, it will merely mean one more Brownie point against my name when I myself am finally wheeled out and deposited on the great rubbish tip up yonder.

No, all I am concerned with is what, precisely, I shall be wheeling out on December 11. "Grey bins are provided by the Council FREE OF CHARGE. However, should you choose to have a green bin, there will be a charge of £4.

Make your request on the Hot Line listed below."

I thought about this for a while. I dialled the number. It was an answering machine. It said: "This is the Wheelbin Office . . ." But it did not tell me what I wanted to know. So I telephoned the Summers Lane Refuse Depot, which owned a human being, and when I asked the human being why it was extra for green, she said: "Well, the green bin is a sort of a, well, status symbol, I suppose."

A *status* symbol? Oh, Barnet, what have we come to? Who, of all those of you whose salary I help to pay, arrives at such conclusions? It it is, as I suspect, Mr A. G. Williams, he need not have wasted time reminding me on page six that "brickbats MUST NOT be placed in the bin".

Because I know exactly what to do with a brickbat.

Urban Gorilla

At a little after 6 pm last Saturday, I was simmering in a sandalwood bath, a chilled vodkatini at my shoulder, a cheroot at my lip, a hysterical Radio 4 political correspondent in one wired ear, and idly speculating upon how long it might be, on present form, before I was summoned from Cricklewood-les-deux-Eglises to form a government, when, in the unplugged ear, the doorbell rang.

The tradition in our house being that, provided I am in the bath and therefore reasonably close to several flights of stairs, there is no point in anyone else walking across the hall to the front door, it was the work of a moment, after the third tocsin had usefully dislodged the looser roof-tiles, to

93

spring from the tub, struggle into a bathrobe which would then be conveniently pre-soaked when I next needed it, and hobble downstairs.

There was a gorilla on the step.

I exaggerate. You cannot call anything three feet tall a gorilla, even if it has a full-grown head on it. What could this be but some hapless experimental mutant which had taken it on the lam and was now bent on sanctuary from the researchers at its heels? God alone knew what it might be from the neck down. It had a sheet on. We stared at one another. It was clearly as nonplussed as I was.

"Triggle," it said, after a bit. Its lips did not move.

Since my command of Simian is scant, I could do no better than respond with: "I'm sorry?"

"He said 'Trick or Treat?'" cried a distant voice. I peered into the darkness beyond. The gale was blowing our beech tree back and forth across the street-light, so that the woman at the far end of our path came and went in sodium glimpses. All very unsettling, even though pennies now began, albeit slowly, to fall.

"But it isn't Hallowe'en yet," I said to the gorilla.

The gorilla turned towards its mother, revealing, rather poignantly, the piece of elastic holding its face on.

"He can't come out Tuesday night," shouted the woman at the gate, who was now invisible again. "He's got school Wednesday morning."

She said this quite sharply, as if to bring home to me the fact that the gorilla had put itself to considerable trouble to ring my bell at all.

The gorilla turned back again, and looked at me.

"Hang on," I said, clenching my teeth against that chatter which tends to follow the collision of a Force 9 breeze with sodden shins, "I'll find something."

I went back inside, rooted around in the larder, found a Mars bar, sloshed back across the hall, and offered it to the gorilla. He did not take it. Instead, the mask motionlessly mumbled something even more incomprehensible than

94

before. "He doesn't seem to want it," I shouted towards the gate.

"What is it?"

"A Mars bar."

"He's not supposed to have chocolate," said the voice from the gloom.

What was he supposed to have? Sushi? Mango? *Cotelette de veau à la manière de la Vicomtesse de Bragalonne?*

"What would you like instead?" I said.

At this, the gorilla – who had clearly arrived at the conclusion that the moment had come to put away childish things – disentangled a small hand from the sheet, put its thumb beneath its plastic chin, and lifted the mask enough to allow intelligible negotiation.

"Can I have fifty pee?" it said.

So I plodded back upstairs, and I got the coin, and I came down and gave it to him, and the sheet flitted quickly up the path like The Woman in White because time was money, and I climbed the stairs again, and the bath was cold and the vodka was warm and the cheroot had gone out and the news was over, so I pulled the plug, and, as I did so, the first banger of Guy Fawkes' Night went off, eight days early.

The kid will doubtless be back next Saturday, with a crayoned sack in a pram. And the Saturday after that, with three bars of "Oh Come All Ye Faithful". I just hope John Major, if it's still him, has got inflation under control by then. If not, it could well be a quid next time.

NOVEMBER

Another Nasty Turn

I wish this page were a wooden cupboard. With my face at the top, but behind a grille, concealing my shame while leaving my lips free for confession. I need absolution. I have done a bad thing.

Late last night – it is Monday as I write – I was plumping cushions, decanting ashtrays, piling Sunday newspapers, opening windows to cool the still-simmering television, and generally winding up the long day's doings, when I felt the premises tremble. Only very slightly, and to a distant rumble: much, I imagine, as England's looser casements and latches are reported to have reacted when the Somme barrage opened up. I looked at my watch, and it was 1.05 am.

That is what reassured me; for we live in interesting times, and it is important for the retiring head to know that it can lower itself to the pillow without pressing concern for terrorist bombs, collapsing tower blocks, imploding sewers, falling aircraft, or any other of the thousand unnatural shocks that contemporary flesh is heir to.

Because it was 1.05 am, I knew it was Leoni from Milan.

Possibly to Milan. Either way, I knew it was Leoni, because 1.05 am, give or take a minute, was when he had come past last Sunday, and the Sunday before that. And I knew his name was Leoni, just as I knew he was Milanese, because, when I lurched out of bed the first time and peered through the curtains, that is what was written on what he was dragging behind him, which was some 30 tons and 60 feet, at a guess, of trailered container-truck.

I didn't hear the approaching rumble the first time, because I was asleep. I remained asleep until Leoni booted his air-brakes for the corner on which we live, but it was not merely the exhaled hiss that woke me, it was the bit of grit that Leoni had picked up in one of his umpteen brake-drums, going up Shap Fell perhaps, or over the Brenner, or wherever it was that Leoni's intercontinental plying took him, and which, brought now to our quiet Cricklewood corner, set clanging all the fillings in the snoring gob like so many tiny fire-alarms.

But last night, I was up and dressed, I had heard Leoni's rumble on the hill and, by the time he was braking for the turn, I was halfway up the front path. Ours is a narrow suburban by-way, with big red circles fore and aft banning the nocturnal passage of anything over 5T, and Leoni owed me an explanation.

As I reached the gate, however, I saw that Leoni had not merely paused for the corner, he was stuck on it. The first section of his juggernaut had turned into the junction, but a skip at the kerb was preventing its straightening out; in order to give himself a wider turning circle, he would have to back up, but the rear of the latter section was already close to parked cars on the driver's side.

As Leoni's door opened and he climbed down to assess the situation, I knew what was going to happen; it was too late to stop it happening; it was too late to duck and run; it was too late, in short, to avoid Leoni's stranded eye.

The eye approached, at a canter, and the lamplight revealed it to be brimming with relief. Leoni shook my hand, while his free arm, waving at the lorry, described what

100

his vocabulary clearly wasn't up to. There was no point in my observing that he shouldn't have bloody been there in the first place, the words would have merely wasted their sweetness on the desert air. So I took the station astern, and saw him back and forth through his ten-point turn, and when he had finally eased himself out of trouble, he jumped down again, and shook my hand again, and it was only then that I pointed to where his headlamps were highlighting the red circle with the little black lorry in it and the 5T injunction, but it was too late. For Leoni interpreted this not merely as my little joke, but as a bond between conspirators of the night, collaborators who subverted the status quo while duller men slept. We were rum-runners, maquisards, brothers.

So he laughed, and I laughed, and he waved from his departing cab, and I waved back, and this morning I went into West Hampstead police station and I said can you do anything about this bastard who drives a juggernaut down my street every Sunday night? and they said have you got his registration number? and I said yes, and I gave it to them, and now I feel terrible.

Half Nelson

Commemoratively speaking, today is a big day. But, commemoratively speaking, it cannot be spoken. It does not have a name. Sadder yet, it does not have *the* name.

The day's candidature for a name is, in fact, extraordinarily broad. Many are the titles with which November 3 might quite properly be endowed. It could, for example, be Orbital Mutt Day, since this was the day upon which, in 1957, the hapless dog Laika was strapped aboard Sputnik II and catapulted into the void. Nor, this being the day immediately following that on which Britain's first motorway was inaugurated in 1959, does National Contraflow Day have an unappealing ring.

One might also stumble – quite literally – across well-wishers celebrating International Coke Day, given that it was at this juncture in 1903 that Panama gained that independence from Colombia which the good General Noriega currently appears determined to rescind, although some of us might be loath to afford immortal honour to a man so bent on sticking his business into other people's noses.

Especially when another contender is a clear half a length up, as it were, on the field. Because it was exactly 146 years ago, on November 3, 1843, that the nether 50 per cent of Lord Nelson was lovingly attached to a block and tackle and winched to the top of his smart new column, to the loyal choral accompaniment of 20,000 cricking necks.

Now, for those of you poised to echo Ronald Reagan's poignant cry as to what happened to the rest of him, the fact is that the little admiral's top half did not join his legs until the following day. As this was the bit with Horatio's identifying features on it (not to mention Horatio's identifying lack of features, here and there), the delay must have meant an unsettling 24 hours for concerned Londoners who knew not only that the public subscription had already run out, but also that the government was still dithering about making good the difference. Would Nelson get his other half at all? Might not some ghastly millionaire cotton-broker gallop opportunistically down from Rochdale with the fiscal shortfall and a granite torso of his own, leaving Ackroyd's Kutprice Kretonne Square in his subsequent wake?

And yet, and yet. For every worrier who gazed up through the flocks of immigrating pigeons, must there not also have been a hundred wags? I offer this not just because all topless stone legs are farcical of themselves, but because, a century-and-a-half on, do we not hear the cockney cackling of innumerable off-colour jokes concerning both the bits that were blown off Nelson and the bits that weren't? As the comedians put their pocket telescopes to their own good eyes and scanned the close-fitting granite hosiery above, would the name Emma not have sprung instantly to the irreverent lip?

Nor, I dare to fancy, would the ghost have given a fig. Even had William IV not put him down as "the merest boy of a captain I ever beheld", there is much in the chronicles of Nelson's behaviour to suggest an engagingly immature daftness, seen to never more telling effect than in that imperishable monocular jape off Copenhagen. Furthermore, like a somewhat unbraver English hero, Horatio was not only witty in himself, but the cause that wit was in other men. Who could fail to love him for his legacy of innuendo? Ask any cricketer why a score of 111 is a Nelson, or any chippie what he calls his screwdriver. Reflect on what Horatio's terminal bunting has done for music-hall ambiguity.

I should give a lot to have been there 146 years ago, where the trunkless legs stood equidistant from Buckingham Palace and 10 Downing Street. Did Queen Victoria and Sir Robert Peel stare from their respective windows at the great column with Nelson's dapper pins atop, and if they did, how were their faces? Po? Chortling? Reflective?

Were they, in short, taking on board the final message that the admiral, or half of him at least, was flagging to posterity from his plinth, getting it in sharpish before the rest of him arrived to be topped out with pomp and sobbing and it was all too late to cock a snook above the tide of reverence?

Or broach the grog for Ozymandias Day.

103

Didn't Hear a Peep

Any Cricklewood villain plucking the final sliver of cod batter from this page before hanging up his bib, depegging his stocking mask, and plimsolling off to earn his living, would be well advised to read on. My house is now protected by an earhole.

Chummy rings my doorbell at his peril. Any fraudulent password muttered on the step, any tell-tale pulmonary quirk (asthmatic wheeze, Woodbine cough, involuntary habitual sniff) will be taken down and may be used in evidence. And let him be further warned that when it comes to phonetics, I am there with Henry Higgins. Within minutes of any attempted break-in, police throughout the land will be on the qui vive for, say, a bronchial Liverpudlian known to have spent several years in Melbourne.

It was not, when I started work on it last Saturday, going to be an earhole. It was going to be a Chubb Door Viewer. Alerted by an article pointing out that London house-holders have an annual one in 20 chance of having their houses held by someone else for long enough to fill a sack, I ran my eye down the checklist of recommended security devices and found that in my case one was conspicuously missing.

This stunned me. How had I overlooked it? An assiduous neurotic, I had over the years painstakingly, not to say cash-takingly, fitted the premises with every possible deterrent. Our external doors are so bright with assorted escutcheons that the chests of none but the most successful Soviet generals would stand comparison, our internal ones so disfigured with brass knobs, bolts, catches and patent devices as to appear to be making some recherché decor statement. Some days, I stand outside a room for a bit, wondering whether it is worth all the bother of getting into it, and go somewhere else. As for the windows, it is as impossible to get out as to get in, so diverse are the locking systems and so untraceably dispersed their various keys.

All these are linked to an alarm system probably unparalleled in its sensitivity. A sudden change in the weather, a bee uncircumspect enough to ignore the photo-electric web, a major sneeze two streets away, will not only set a half dozen bells jolting the crockery off its shelves but, connected as I am to the Metropolitan switchboard, send every alert copper within a 50-mile radius keenly hurtling to his typewriter to begin the long process of triplicating those requisition forms necessary to release his whistle from the safe.

And yet, somehow, I had never thought of fitting a spy hole. Once thought, however, there was no gainsaying the fitting, and I was alongside the Robert Dyas counter in a trice. "It's a solid door," I said. "They don't make them like that any more."

"You want a ws13," said Robert.

In another trice I was back home, drill in one hand, instructions in the other. *1. Mark position of viewer on outside of door. Drill 13 mm hole.* I did this. The drill went into the door surprisingly easily. That was because it did not go through the door. I discovered this when I looked at the inside of the door and found it intact. The door was not solid at all. It was made of two sheets, fitted either side of a frame. It was hollow in the middle. The any more they didn't make them like began longer ago than I had thought.

This meant I would have to mark position of viewer on *inside* of door and drill 13 mm hole. I did this. I now had two 13 mm holes. However, when I looked through one, I did not see the other. In order to align them, I should have to

make the outside one a little bit larger. Just a little bit.
Enough say, so that when I implemented 2. *Locate viewer in
drilled hole*, the viewer would discover that the hole was
perhaps a billimetre larger than its retaining lip, enabling it
effortlessly to disappear. I now had a viewer in my door, all
right. I had it in the bottom of my door. I confirmed this by
opening and closing the door quickly, so that it made the
noise of a viewer rolling about.

I put someone outside and looked through the hole. I
could see part of a nose. A hole was not enough. How could
it be? Chubb were not born yesterday.

Still, I am, as I said, ahead of the game. Since Saturday, I
have been able to hear everything said on the step. Up until
now, it has mainly been "Why have they got a hole in the
door?", but it is early days yet.

Eye Society

It is called Eyeland. Of course it is. The time is 1989, the
place is Colindale Enterprise Zone, the architecture is
post-Legoist, the colours are primary, the towering
ribbed-aluminium neighbours are Kwikfit and MFI and
Do-It-All. What else would it be called? Well, Eyepermar-
ket, possibly, Eurospex, I suppose, or even Just Looking;
but Eyeland is what they have plumped for.

As I drove in, the emblazoned portal unquestionably
exuded theme-park jollity. Might there be performing eyes
at 11.30 and 2.30? Synchronized rolling, say, or breathtaking
feats of high-wire speed-reading by Hungarian tumblers;

106

perhaps a couple of dolphins putting one another's contact lenses in and a conjuror producing glass eyes from kiddies' ears? The heart raced.

I slotted cannily into a corner of the vast car park, a brick wall to starboard, a steel rail astern – in a spot where all the drivers had come because they needed glasses, it seemed circumspect to expose as few flanks as possible – and I walked along the 50-yard run of window, dressed with fashion plates of the begoggled glamorous: here a young gigolo lolling against the bonnet of his white XR3i, there a lantern-jawed powerbroker glinting from his Jag, beside them a selection of international nubilia gazing softly from Riviera balconies, and all of them, of course, shimmeringly enhanced. Not, mind, by spectacles; for there are no spectacles in Eyeland.

Only eyewear.

Nor does this eyewear come in ranges; it comes in collections. The Owl Centenary Collection, The Porsche Carrera Collection, The Classic Collection for Pensioners. These are not bins at all, runs the sub-text, these are not prostheses for the optically crumbling, these are works of art for the connoisseur. Acquaintances cursed with 20–20 vision will gnash their teeth at their misfortune, not only when they clock the masterpiece straddling your conk, but when, invited to the unveiling of your latest prize, they stand before your Chippendale display-cabinet, wincing as envy turns the Beluga to ashes in their mouths.

I arrived, eventually, at the doors, which sighed automatically open. As they were bound to do; the last thing Eyeland's image could risk was discerning collectors bouncing off the plate glass, as if there were something wrong with their eyesight.

Inside, Magritte had been at work. Inside, rank upon rank of eyeless eyewear stared down at you from spotlit galleries. The lower tiers stared up at you. It was the kind of unsettling scrutiny you normally get only in catacombs. I moved uneasily towards the centre of this arena, and fetched up beneath The Roland Rat Collection, where a svelte girl in black, who had detached herself from a murmuring school of such, intercepted me.

"I understand you have off-the-peg reading glasses at £14.95," I said.

I know that look. I encountered its twin when I once asked for an EPNS jam-spoon in Asprey's.

"When did you last have an eye test?" she said.

"Three years ago," I said.

So she took my head and plugged it into a machine that puffed air in my eyes (this alone well worth the £10.40) and another machine that clacked out a computerized prescription, and then she passed me to a charming man who said that the computer print-out was a load of rubbish, and launched into an hour of dedicated testing, to include a complete history of my habits and hobbies, at the end of which he declared that it beat him why men who were prepared to fork out £1,000 on a set of golf clubs blanched at buying a set of eyewear. What I needed, it seemed, was a mashie for reading, a niblick for the VDU, a putter for DIY, a bifocal driver for angling, and so on.

Doubtless, were I to have one of my fuller days, their Designer Department would be happy to provide me with a lizard-skin Gucci bandoliero for carrying my enormous eyewear collection about in.

"I suppose £14.95 would be out of the question?" I murmured.

How often cheap fiction provides the *mot juste*! A mocking grin played about his mouth. A hollow laugh issued from his throat.

So I agreed to begin my collection with reading-glasses, and let me tell you my new eyewear is terrific. The bill for £187.50 is as clear as anything.

Refusniks

I should not have come to Hampstead Garden Suburb by car. I should have come by Lysander. Parachute, even. Landed in the field behind Institute Hall last Monday night, lain in the sodden grass, waited for the local *maquisards* to scuttle, crouching, out of the chilly fog, shaken hands silently, mouthed the password.

Wheelbin.

It is a long way from Cricklewood to Hampstead Garden Suburb. It is halfway across Occupied Barnet. Could be another country: Cricklewood is mean, raunchy, cynical, urbane, tough. Cricklewood ducks and dives. Hampstead Garden Suburb is gentle, demure, idealistic, suburbane, mild. Hampstead Garden Suburb nods and smiles.

But common enemies bring common cause. When, three weeks ago, this column fulminated against the decision by Barnet Waffen SS to impose, willy-nilly, the Wheeled Dustbin Scheme, it little realized it was not alone in its determination to resist. It did not know about The Hampstead Garden Suburb Residents' Association. Cricklewood does not have such things. When a Cricklewood Resident suspects that a fast one is being pulled, his recourse consists of slipping a horseshoe into his glove.

The moment the letter from the HGSRA Chairman arrived, I could tell I was dealing with a different class of person. That Mrs Whelan did not refer to herself as Person, indeed, indicated much. Nor did the enclosed pamphlet exactly threaten a reign of revolutionary terror – PUBLIC

109

MEETING: HOW TO MITIGATE THE IMPACT OF
WHEELIE BINS ON THE SUBURB.
  Hope slowed in mid-ascent.
  Note "wheelie"; could anything bespeak gentility more?
With one coy syllable, a trash can had been anthropomor-
phized. It would have its own TV series next. Rod Hull and
Wheelie. Note "mitigate the impact"; what a hostage to
fortune that is! Do we not hear them hooting in the Barnet
Führerbunker? Be sure that if Cricklewood had a Residents'
Association, it would have rejected HANG THE BAS-
TARDS NOW! as weak-kneed compromise.
  Nevertheless, I went. But it was as I had feared. A huge
audience of nice people. Reasonable people. Fairly elderly
people, too, since a quarter of Garden Suburbanites, as the
speakers constantly pled, are pensioners. In vain I scruti-
nized the ranks of overcoating for a gleam of leather, a flash
of stud. But the sticks they carried did not have big nails on
the end; they had big rubber caps. What, with such forces at
her shoulder, could the chairman do except go not for the
council's jugular, but its heart? So that my own, as her
eloquence directed itself at the plight of the aged and infirm
and the aesthetic doom trundling towards each honeysuck-
led porch, sank. Rebellions cannot be built on pathos, nor
tyrannies overturned by reason.
  I took a last look round, in the fond hope that a few
stubbled pyschopaths, held up perhaps by the need to oil
their Brens, had come in behind me, but there was no one
save a frail cove poking a Fisherman's Friend through a gap
in his muffler, so I left. As I closed the door, a voice from the
dais was murmuring, gently, that time for protest was
running out.
  It little knew how fast.
  The morrow dawn, the fog not yet lifted, I was woken by a
drear clanking. I did not need to bother the curtains; the
rising gooseflesh told me all. It remembered Prague. The
Barnet bins were rolling in. We had been caught napping.
When I did look out, the street was deserted. No weeping

women pressed flowers into the invaders' hands, no shouting students chucked themselves beneath their wheels; it was all too late for that. At every gate, a wheelbin stood, grey as the fog.

I ran downstairs, in time to catch the emptied lorry at the corner. It had *Plastic Omnium* stencilled on its flank. What was Plastic Omnium? Some remote star? But four seeming-human beings stared from the cab.

"What's going on?" I cried. "These aren't due till December 11."

"Don't ask me, cock," said the driver. "We're from Telford."

Not like Prague, then; like Peking. To do their dirty work, Barnet had drummed up mercenaries from a remote and alien province. Not for Barnet, Europe's wind of change.

I may move to Leipzig.

Dead and Berried

I'll say this for me, there can't be many other butlers prepared to slog through *The Golden Bough* in the line of duty. Especially ones who are no less willing to spend an entire Monday morning phoning tree surgeons, following a Sunday spent shinning up and down a rickety ladder, simply in order to lay a lunch-table five weeks hence. Also get a flea in the ear from the Italian consulate.

It beats me why the Italian consular service should think it has better things to do than find out what the Roman

111

weather was like two millennia ago. They must have charts, somewhere. It is surely only a question of running a finger along the basement shelves.

What I was trying to discover was whether, when Romans had their in-laws over for Saturnalia Day lunch, exchanged tartan *crepidae* three sizes too large, listened to the Emperor's speech, got plastered, yelled at the kids, and all that, the holly on their tables had berries on it.

I admit there was an element of wool-gathering here – it is an occupational hazard which afflicts the most serious of researchers; I had even sidetracked myself into wondering how the Romans ever played charades: so few books, so little drama, no films or television at all, can't keep on miming *The Eclogues* year after year – but it sprang from serious thoughts as to whether Rome had once been colder than Cricklewood. I might, who knows, have added a major footnote to the greenhouse debate.

That the Romans decked their halls with boughs of ilex there was no question: all there in *The Golden Bough* along with many another of Frazer's unsettling examples of Christian plagiarism. What I wanted to know was whether the ilex had berries on.

I should never have asked the question had this not been a big year for our holly tree. It was the year the tree finally lost its virginity. I planted it when we moved in 18 years before, so that at least one of the things I should otherwise have to run around paying through the nose for on Christmas Eve would be taken care of, but until this year I had had no such luck. The tree got bigger, but it never got pregnant.

This was a source of great sadness to me. For the ilex, as you know, is dioecious: its sexual habits are impeccably unsolitary, it will engage in vegetable nookie only if the right partner comes along, and, heartbreakingly, this never happened to ours. It just stood there by the fence, year after year, a great green gawky wallflower, when even the wallflowers were cross-pollinating like knives. Nobody even asked whether it came here often.

Which has meant that every December 24 I have had to

112

cough up for berried sprigs, because you can't deck a hall with sterile holly. It ends up looking like a funeral parlour.

But this year, all that changed: the tree got lucky. I know neither how nor when, certainly none of us heard anything and we're all light sleepers, but at some point, in the hitherto passionless bed by the back fence, the earth moved. With the happy result that in early September the tree suddenly burgeoned with hundreds of fat red by-blows. Almost embarrassing, but hugely cheering. Not only should I have tablesful of the stuff, I should be able to bundle it up for those in need. It even crossed my mind to bundle it up for those in funds: I could hire a barrow and a cloth cap, trundle the streets crying some fetchingly Dickensian cry . . .

Last Sunday, as I was exhuming a rotted rhizome, something fell on my head. I looked up, and something fell in my eye. When I looked down again, I saw a number of wrinkled berries. I got the ladder. It was not a pretty sight. Shrivel never is.

Next day, all six tree surgeons said the same. The long hot summer, whose restless nights may well have played their part in knocking the holly up, had also served to advance its season. "What can I do?" I said. "Dunno," said the surgeon. So I phoned Kew.

"You can't do anything for the tree," said Kew, "but if you want berried sprigs at Christmas, cut them off now, and squirt them with hairspray."

They didn't specify ozone-friendly, but it went without saying. Who knows, maybe the stuff the Romans sprayed on theirs explains why mine has warmed up now?

I might have found out, if the Italians hadn't hung up.

DECEMBER

Panda Cars

I used to suck trucks.

This almost certainly accounts for a number of unfortunate later developments, including the fact that my memory is not what it was. I sucked trucks in the days before anyone knew that lead knocked out brain cells. If I had never sucked trucks, I should no doubt, today, be able to remember all the trucks I didn't suck. As it is, I can remember only two trucks I did suck, a black Jowett 10cwt, and a somewhat larger green pantechnicon belonging to Carter Paterson. That is to say, it had "Carter Paterson" stencilled across its rear doors; it actually belonged to me. After a while, mind, it had "art erso" stencilled across its rear doors, because that is what major sucking can do to a truck.

The Jowett van is probably worth real money now, because it must have been painted with suck-resistant material. The day I sold it, it still had Allen & Hanbury's Pastilles stencilled down the sides, in pristine blue, and not a serif eroded. These days they fetch a lot at auction, if they're mint (condition, not flavour), and I wish I'd hung on to it, because what I sold it for was a Bakelite telescope with 2x

117

magnification. At least that's what David Collingwood claimed it had; I spent some hours with one eye peering through it and the other open for comparison and to this day I remain unconvinced that the telescope could do better than 1x. If, indeed, that: I could never get the Standard Telephone Works to look anything but smaller, whichever end I looked through. This was particularly irritating, because the Standard Telephone Works was the main reason I had swapped the Jowett van in 1944: many of us were convinced that Standard Telephone was engaged in manufacturing secret weapons, which a decent telescope might have revealed.

I wasn't still sucking trucks in 1944, of course. David Collingwood got a bone-dry Jowett. I never sucked trucks after 1940, because by that time I had learned to push them along. But before then I used to take vehicles to bed, despite the fact that in December 1938, when I was six months old, the London Zoo acquired three pandas called Ming, Tang and Sung, just in time for the Christmas market. With the result that most kids of my age sucked pandas.

I tell you all this because without it you would be at a loss to understand why I am, this morning, well-nigh inconsolable. I would be at a loss to understand it myself, had I not spent some hours dredging stuff up from the bottom of the psyche's murky sump. Which, sifted and labelled, leads me to believe that I still think of certain vehicles not merely as cuddly toys but as pets. As a child, not only did I never have a panda, I never had a pet – possibly because both my parents were animal-lovers, and with the Stuka-clouds gathering over Europe didn't want to bring a puppy into a world like that – and I am now convinced that this was the function which the Jowett served. Had I been able to talk when it arrived, I might well have christened it Spot. We shall probably never know.

What we do know is that my inconsolability this morning derives from my having to have a vehicle put to sleep. Readers brought up on a lead-free diet may have enough memory to recall a 1972 Austin 1100 I bought almost a year ago, to tide me over until a newly ordered car arrived. I never got rid of it. I could not. I did not have the heart. It was Old Shep. It sat under the beech-tree outside, and whenever I took the new car out of the garage Old Shep gave off the kind of mute reproach that Walt Disney would have put under instant contract. So from time to time I drove it about a bit. Things dropped off – it was, after all, 85 in human terms – but sheer guts kept it going. Old Shep was all heart.

But not much else. Last week, I took it for its MOT, and a number of grown men fell about, and that was it. Old Shep had terminal rust. Old Shep would have to be scrapped. I had never had to put a car down before. I took it to three scrapyards. Terrible places. Limbs and organs everywhere. Finally, a man gave me a fiver, and I got a cab home for six. Even as I write, I stare at the void beneath the beech, just in case Old Shep escapes and finds his way home, limping.

Why couldn't they have bought me a panda?

Points in Cricklewood's Favour

Small towns do not make history; they wait for history to make them. Like Blanche Du Bois – a sylvan hamlet in the Auvergne, if I remember aright, twinned with Williams, Tennessee – they have always depended upon the kindness of strangers. Bethlehem, Gettysburg, Kittyhawk, Agincourt, Los Alamos, Ladysmith, Yalta, lie drowsing on the misty banks of the River Lethe until, willy-nilly, they are suddenly awoken by the midnight rap of destiny's knuckle, and by dawn you cannot hear yourself speak for the ringing of the souvenir-mongers' tills.

Last Monday, British Rail submitted a Bill to Parliament concerning further plans for the Channel tunnel. Now, while enshrined within it is what will surely be welcome, if minor, recognition for a number of hitherto anonymous villages – there are to be passing loops at Headcorn, Otford, and Borough Green, not to mention a major junction at Bickley – there is no question but that the nub of this document, and the fulcrum of the mighty communications system it addresses, is a new half-mile rail link at a place called West End Lane.

This is very possibly the first time any of you has heard of West End Lane – unless, of course, your ringlets are coiffed by Bojangles For Hair, or your clogs are cobbled by Mr Minit, or your liver is undermined by The Grog Blossom – but were you to walk to my front gate and throw a reasonably aerodynamic stone, there is a fair chance that someone in West End Lane would cry "Ow!"

For West End Lane is the jewel of South Cricklewood: it lies equidistant between Shoot Up Hill and Finchley Road, bonding their two great hinterlands together with all the sophisticated glitter of dried Uhu. And now, thanks to its fortuitous position athwart the Sheffield–St Pancras and North London lines (currently feeding Fenchurch Street, St Pancras, Moorgate, Liverpool Street, King's Cross, Euston, Marylebone, Paddington and Waterloo), yet greater glory beckons. Because South Cricklewood is to be nothing less than the British nexus of Eurolink. Heathrow on rails.

Small wonder that local hats flew in the air at the collapse of international communism: the new mobility following in freedom's wake will mean that, as soon as the requisite digging and making good is done, a man will be able to walk into the Vladivostock ticket office and ask for a cheap return to Cricklewood, and there will be nothing to interrupt his course, except perhaps frost on the points at Ashford. Such tourists could very well be big spenders: though the phrase "much-needed roubles" has yet to trouble the *FT*s typeset-

120

ters, the Cricklewood economy has never been one to look a gift horse in the mouth, and I am assured by the chatelaine of Jason's Fish Bar that a Russian able to cough up nothing more than the wherewithal for a bag of chips and a pickled gherkin would not be shown the door.

Conversely, when mulching palls and the crossword's done and there's nothing on but *Very Nearly the Best of the Two Ronnies Again*, I shall be able to throw a few toiletries into a carpet-bag, stroll into the South Cricklewood concourse, pluck a credit card from my wallet, and, in little more than two shakes of a brakeman's pennant, join the fashionable *vien-et-vont* along the Odessa promenade. If, that is, something better doesn't crop up *en route*: as E. Phillips Oppenheim and Graham Greene would be only too ready to bear witness, a thousand miles of permanent way can be a funny old Johnny, and should a sloe-eyed heiress burst into my sleeper on the grounds that the bloke with the ermine spats and the duelling scar who got on at Bratislava means her no good at all, I may not be answerable for my response.

Yestermorning, I strolled down to the present Cricklewood Station to test the wind. It is a rum building, in Victorian pest-house style, with a hand-written placard tied to its bent railing saying "Cash paid for unwanted coke, please ring . . .", and at the moment the furthest you can get from it without changing is Purley, but I have every confidence that when the great Euroday dawns, history's balance shall not find it wanting.

I mean, you'd never believe the state Gatwick was in, once upon a time.

Prepare to Shed Them Now

Since the first weekend in December is traditionally the time when the meticulous gardener prepares his mower for winter storage by placing it on blocks (taking care to position sump over drip pan), draining engine oil and flushing, loosening and greasing all nuts and bolts against seizure, checking magneto points, easing cutting cylinder, removing chain-case and lubricating chain, extracting spark-plug and sandpapering all traces of carbon before putting in safe dry place, checking and oiling all cutting surfaces, brushing out dried vegetable matter, cleaning air filter with white spirit, and liberally applying Elastoplast to all gashes not requiring professional suturing, I went down to the shed on Saturday, had a quick shufti at it through the window, and was just about to stroll back to the house in the satisfaction of a job well done, when, half-way up the path, I stopped.

I know that shed. I know everything that is in it, and where everything that is in it is. You either have a tidy mind or you haven't. I know exactly where each old trowel-handle and sliver of rotted stake and dried-out creosote-tin is strewn, I know exactly where the piles of worm-eaten tubers and coagulated potting compost and rusted fruit-spray nozzles have lain these many years past, and by the same token I know exactly when something is lying there which these many years past hasn't been. That is why I stopped half-way up the path, because, though the glance inside had been as cursory as any in my repertoire, something untoward had nevertheless had time to emboss itself on the retina. I went back.

On the floor, between half a deck-chair and a deflated football, was a tortoise. Not necessarily a whole tortoise – a less experienced eye than mine would quite probably have registered two deflated footballs, and strolled on – but certainly the carapace. I went into the shed, and bent down, and behold! it was indeed a whole tortoise. The working bits were inside. It had done the thing that tortoises do.

The shed-door having been warped ajar since – was it 1976 when I assembled it? – the tortoise had clearly, at the first snap of frost, crept inside for its winter kip. At this thought, I felt a warm glow of my own: animals in straitened circumstances knew instinctively where to turn. Had Assisi not beaten us to the draw, Cricklewood might well have found itself in the calendar of saints. My second thought was to pull down a piece of mildewed sacking from the nail on which it had been hanging for some years on the now totally vindicated grounds that I might never know when I needed it, and swaddle the visitor.

After which I went into the house for paper and pencil. A note on the gate was called for. Cricklewood is not, after all, a byword for its chelonian fauna, and out there some grief-stricken child would even now be poking frantically about its premises looking for something to put in the straw-filled shoe-box it had so lovingly prepared against a nipping and an eager air. Nice big note, and pretty soon the neighbourhood would echo to ringing cries of "He's found Tommy, he's found Tommy!"

"What's that?" said my wife, as the note and I passed her in the hall. I explained.

"You're sure it's not dead?" she said.

I looked at her for a bit. Then I went back to the shed. I lifted the sacking. This was not going to be easy. Had it been a cat or a hamster, I should have known right off. Its chest would have been going up and down. Its whiskers would have been doing things. But how do you tell if a tortoise is breathing? You cannot even see its nostrils. If it is hibernating and you wake it up to see whether it is alive, the shock could kill it. I put the note back in my pocket. Not only did I not wish to raise false hopes, I did not wish the neighbourhood to echo to ringing cries of "He's killed Tommy, he's killed Tommy!"

Instead, I rang Regent Pet Stores. What professionals they are! Do not look for mawkish nonsense in Camden Town. They probably never miss *Bambi*. Takes you out of yourself, a good laugh.

"Try sniffing it," said the caring person on the other end. "It'll tell you right away whether it's dead or not."

I haven't been back to the shed. It will, after all, be spring in a few months. No rush with the note.

Off the Peg

By the time you read this, I might be almost anywhere. I might be standing in the Parkhurst slopping-out queue; I might be attached to one of the Middlesex Hospital's fine ceilings by an intricate system of ropes and pulleys; I might be facing an apoplectic clubman through the dawn mist of Hyde Park and wondering what it feels like to be spitted on a sabre; I might even be slumped over a Fort Zinderneuf embrasure, twitching occasionally as a Tuareg sniper finds his mark.

If, that is, I am not walking up and down Garrick Street.

Wherever I am, *The Times* will be to blame. Last Wednesday, *The Times* threw an elegant bash at the Garrick

Club so that the vast diaspora of hacks who do not meet from one year to the next could forgather over goblet and chipolata and, in true Yuletide spirit, attempt to ferret out one another's pay and conditions, and a splendid do it was.

I wore my coat. Not inside, of course. If you have a navy cashmere coat, you do not want to wear it at a *Times* party, because you are liable to get vol-au-vent shards all over it. They are an exuberant crowd, and will not stay an anecdote simply because a tray of canapés heaves to alongside, they will carry on barking through the spray; the smart thing is to wear a patterned suit on which fragments of prawn do not show, and which you can shake clean by stamping up and down outside the members' cloakroom, before putting your navy cashmere coat on again.

If it is still there.

I did not immediately know it was not still there. The reason I did not know it was not still there has much to do with the reason why it wasn't. I had arrived early at the party, and mine was the first coat on the line of pegs, but when I moved to leave, there were thirty identical coats hanging there. When I put on the one which was on my peg, I found that it had a roll of Trebor mints in one pocket, and a little rubber grommet in the other, possibly an ear-plug.

You would be astonished at what Garrick clubmen have in their pockets. You would not believe the range of emergencies for which they prepare themselves before walking abroad. Even I know only the half of it, because I had got as far as coat 17 – a set of miniature screwdrivers in a plastic wallet and a single tartan sock – when a chap passed me on his way to the gents' and asked if he could help, in that tone of voice by which extremely civil people imply that Bow Street nick is only a holler away.

I explained, and he very kindly went and brought the porter, so that they could both look at me for a bit. I told the porter that what I had in my pocket was a packet of Silk Cut, and we both went at it; but the coat had clearly gone. The porter said it would be bound to turn up next morning, when he would telephone. I went home, blowing on my fingers.

It did not turn up on Thursday morning, but as I was going to Rules for lunch anyway, I elected to pass by the Garrick. A lot of navy cashmere coats entered as I stood on the step, but none of them looked as though it was concealing a packet of fags. After lunch, I went back, and a lot of other navy cashmere coats were now emerging, but it was clear that nothing could come of it. You cannot go up to a bloke in the street and ask if you can root around in his pockets.

When it did not turn up on Friday morning, I decided to cut my losses. I phoned Guardian Royal Exchange, and said I wished to make a claim on my all-risks policy. I explained why. The GRE said it would have to go down as theft; had the police been informed? A small cloud formed on my horizon, no bigger than a member's fist. I said I'd ring back. Instead, I rang a couple of member-friends. They went mad. I could not accuse a Garrick member of nicking a measly bloody coat. I would be calumniated, thrashed, ridden out of town on a rail. My only course was to apologize to the porter, own up to an attempted scam for the insurance money, and join the French Foreign Legion. That is what a gentleman did, they said, rather than risk having his friends tarred with his brush and blackballed by the Garrick.

Even asking what I am going to ask may well incur unspeakable reprisal, but I shall ask it anyway: if you are a member of the Garrick, have a feel in your pockets. I don't know what the wind's like where you are, but it's freezing in Cricklewood.

126

By Their Fruits Ye Shall Know Them

I do believe England has changed a bit.

Yesterday morning was not exclusively yesterday morning. Just after 11 o'clock, as the result of a chance eavesdrop, it became, for a brief period, a December evening in 1942. I did not need to close my eyes; I continued to stare at the slope of artificial grass, for cinema has taught us the trick of the dissolve, and in less than a nano-second my father was standing in front of the artificial grass slope, unslinging his gasmask case with one hand and removing his bicycle clips with the other. He then kissed my mother, picked me up – I feel the pressure of his hands in my armpits as I write – walked into the hall, and shut the front door with his foot. The letter-box rattled.

Since he is now beyond the reach of the firing-squad, I feel no qualms in letting the film continue to clatter through the sprockets for a bit. He had come home from RAF Stradishall on a 48-hour pass – as odd as anything else is the thought, now, of anyone cycling the 70 miles to London and the 70 miles back, just for the weekend – but this time he did not hang his gasmask case on the hatstand, as usual; he carried it into the kitchen and put it on the table. As the action was accompanied by a broad smile, I did not, even at four, take this to be a sign that the Luftwaffe was about to start unloading phosgene on Wembley, but I was nevertheless puzzled. My father was a man of inflexible routine.

He then spent an unnecessary amount of time opening the

127

gasmask case, clearly still enjoying himself no end, but when he finally did, he did not lift out his gasmask; he lifted out, very carefully, something wrapped in newspaper. And unwrapped it.

It was a shrunken head. I knew it was a shrunken head, because at Barham Park Primary School the talk in those days was of little else. Japan had been in the war for a year, and it was a well-known fact that the Japanese had entered the fracas only for the unrivalled opportunities it offered to cut people's heads off with long curved swords, and shrink them. I looked at the shrivelled brown ovoid with its ragged top-knot, and felt the goosebumps nudge the flannelled neck. I could not guess how my father had come by it, but I suppose I assumed that the RAF was now engaging the forces of Nippon in close encounter and that an incautious crew-member had poked his head out of a Lancaster turret and paid the price of folly.

I was still speculating on how they had retrieved it – had my old man, or someone else, put down briefly to collect it, had they perhaps flown past at zero feet and, as at an *Ivanhoe* tourney, reached out and snatched it as they sped, had the Japs themselves, perhaps, posted it back to Blighty *pour décourager les autres*? Who knows where this speculation might not have taken me had my mother not, after a moment or two, said: "Just in time for Christmas, too."

I looked at her, since she was not a woman known for her *sang froid*.

"I wouldn't," said my father. "It's pretty ripe now."

So I looked at him, then.

"It's called a pineapple," said my mother, to me. "Where," she said to my father, "did you get it?"

"Long story," said my father.

He told it to me after the war, but I was supposed to keep it under my hat. Though far rarer than the rest, the pineapple was like all the other stuff he used to bring home on leave, the eggs, the butter, the bars of chocolate; he (and I understand he was not the only member of Bomber Command to do so) swapped petrol for them, though

128

smuggling a jerrycan from an RAF station was a capital offence. Had he caught him, Harris would probably have strangled my old man with his bare hands.

But 47 years is a long time, and if no one else will forgive him, I shall. Despite the fact that the pineapple, when my mother cut into it, was brown, liquescent, and extremely nasty.

Which is why all this sprang to mind yesterday, in the greengrocery section of Waitrose. A man came up to the woman beside me, and said: "Right, I got two pounds of lychees, two pounds of passion fruit, a pound of kumquats, half a dozen mangoes, and a couple of nice big paw-paw, but they say they haven't got any breadfruit."

And the woman sniffed, and said: "Typical."

A Night on the Tiles

A t least the whole business had a satisfying circularity about it. That may not be much, but you find yourself seeking such consolations when you are tapping away in the loft and there is someone tapping away above you, and when your eye looks up, it catches his eye looking down. That is not the satisfying circularity, by the way; you will have to hang on for what is, and even then I cannot promise it will be satisfying to you. It is not even that satisfying to me, but, as I say, when you are rooting around for consolation, it is a question of any port in a storm. In this case, literally.

Last night, i.e. Wednesday as I tap, started as a very good

night indeed. It did not grow terrible until it had ceased to be Wednesday, and the circularity came upon it. Wednesday being the former Foreign Secretary's birthday, and the former Foreign Secretary being a much-loved fellow, one of those who much loved him had convened a remarkable binge at Julian Humfrey's Ordinary, a spot which takes great pains to belie its title, for it is in fact the most extraordinary restaurant in London. It has but one table. It has but one meal. That is what gives it its name, as anyone who has trawled p.1461 of the *Shorter Oxford* will testify, having noted that, since 1590, an ordinary has been not only an eating-house which regularly provides a public meal at a fixed price, but also the company that frequents such troughs.

We were an ordinary of 10, sitting on an oval 1726 table in an oval 1726 house and poking a 1726 dinner into our faces, for Mr Humfrey insists upon consistency, and there is nothing on his Spitalfields premises that would not have been there in 1726, when it was built. Or at any rate, there isn't supposed to be, but it isn't too easy to check by candlelight; you count yourself lucky if you have managed to avoid barking your shins on a 1726 chair or leaving an ear on a 1726 wall-bracket without peering at them to see whether they were actually sent round by MFI last Tuesday.

Anyway, many an oyster and many a quail and many a haunch of this and that had been engulleted, to the accompaniment of many a bumper, I believe the word is, of a wine which seemed to have stood the passage of 263 years jolly well, and the former Foreign Secretary was in high spirits, as might be expected of an honest man no longer required to be sent abroad to lie for his country (no jokes later than 1726 today, I'm afraid); and as Wednesday became Thursday, we debouched, rolling slightly, into the night. To discover that a great roaring wind had come up, which was hurling rags of cloud across the moon above Christ Church opposite, and thereby making Hawksmoor's ambivalent masterpiece even more sinister than any church has a licence to be; so that as we clutched our hats and

130

lurched down Fournier Street towards our cabs, we were moved to honk that the eeriness of the weather was making this a very 1726 night indeed, the ghosts were palpable, might that shadow not be tiny Alexander Pope leaning into the gale, could that be Joseph Addison sheltering in the doorway – you know what it's like when you've tied a few on – but what we agreed above all was how fortunate we were to have conservationists among us so passionately committed that Fournier Street had not gone the way of so much else.

I do not know when I got home, nor why, when I arrived, I climbed up to my attic study instead of falling into bed; I know only when I woke up, in my chair (3.46 am) and why (rain falling on head). That is why, when I look up now, I can see Mr Coombs looking down through the hole where the roof-tiles used to be before the storm blew them off.

Mr Coombs is a serious roofer. Arriving at 9, he set out the options in the kind of craft argot of which Mr Humfrey would approve. It was a matter, apparently, of time-worn nibs; there was a simple expedient – patching with bright new tiles – or a complex – re-roofing the entire section with selected old ones.

Complex = simple x 20, where £ is the constant. I hesitated.

"A roof is a beautiful thing," murmured Mr Coombs, "done right." So no option at all, really. Who knows, this might one day be the site of some aspiring ordinary, and I should not like to think of pedantic drunks crawling all over the roof, sniggering at clay anachronisms.

JANUARY

When the Kissing Had to Start

I am not sure, now, how I had originally intended to earmark the decade just gone. It is, of course, not the only thing I am not sure of at this moment, because this moment is a mere eight hours or so into the new decade. I am, for example, not sure of the whereabouts of my other shoe. I am not sure why, each time a type-key detonates upon the platen, a tiny shard of brain shears off and drops, vibrating, somewhere down behind my tonsils. I am not sure how long it will take before I can resume my normal method of igniting a cigarette, instead of holding the lighter stable on the desk in front of me with both hands and slowly inching my head towards the flame until rude, trembling contact is made.

But all this is as you would expect on New Decade's Day, when retribution follows so swiftly upon the excesses of New Decade's Eve that you know that this is nature's way of slipping you a moral object lesson with which to kick off your decennial regeneration. Some of us, of course, have further to trudge down that purgative road than others, and that I suddenly find myself one of them is the part of New

Decade's Day that I did not expect. When, a few short hours ago, the first cork flew out upon its inaugural mission, I fully believed that I should be remembering the 1980s as The Gorbachov Decade or The Botham Decade or The Minogue Decade. How could I have guessed that all such culturally momentous labels as had been jockeying for selection should, on a sudden, fade and curl and fall, and that I should be compelled forevermore to remember the 1980s as the decade when I kissed my first man?

For though it was just after midnight in France it was just after 11pm in England when it happened, and let me tell you that, The Branagh Decade notwithstanding, gentlemen in England then a-bed should think themselves bloody fortunate they were not here, and hold their manhoods dear whiles any speaks that kissed with us upon New Decade's Day.

It had all started so promisingly, too: a crystalline evening in the Riviera foothills, the stars winking off our patent toecaps as our dress shoes rang upon the frosty cobbles, the cheery British honking of our pre-lubricated eightsome bringing the locals scuttling to the windows high above us in ambivalent welcome, nine festive courses waiting to unreel themselves at the finest restaurant in Tourrettes-sur-Loup, the sweet prospect of a bloated stagger homeward to a roaring log – what better accompaniment could one ask for a trip across the decadal divide?

Le Petit Manoir was full, though somewhat po-faced. Thirty *habitants* were shovelling up their crayfish and goose-liver with all the single-mindedness of the napkinned Gaul, and hardly glanced from their crockery as we bounced in. A bit unfestive, but that is because the cracker is unknown in France; which is why we had imported our own. Within seconds of our sitting down, the restaurant was reeling beneath the bang and reek of cordite, the convivial winging of tiny plastic key-rings, the shriek and jest and motto, and the sight – horrifying to any republican – of eight crowned heads firmly attached to the bodies beneath.

To give them their due, they rallied well. By midnight we had got half a dozen crowned, we had explained what was funny about a *poulet* crossing a *rue*, we had received agreement that a fallen streamer could do little to ruin a decent soup. Cordial entente reigned. And then, as midnight struck, the chef appeared, gently raised me from my chair, and proffered his cheek.

"I don't think I can do this," I said to my wife.

"I don't think you have any option," she said.

He had sideburns. I had never felt sideburns on my lips before.

The bloke at the next table had a beard. It was like eating a hedge. The head waiter was wearing the same aftershave as mine: a strange experience. My fourth conquest was tiny and bald, with the result that the most obvious target for my plonker left a sort of condescension in its wake that I fear has botched any chance of a second date.

I got through 14 Frenchmen last night. As for the Englishmen in our party, we sort of eyed one another for a bit, but that was all. Everyone was a bit quiet walking home, I thought.

Knowing the Drill

"Look up 'twinge'," I said. She opened the dictionary again. While I waited, I moved a threatening fragment of croissant across the roof of my mouth with the tip of my tongue, gingerly, and deposited it carefully on the safe side. She finished flipping.

"*Elancement*," she said, finally. "Or possibly *remords*. I shouldn't think it's *remords*, though. *Remords* sounds like conscience."

"On the other hand," I said, "*élancement* sounds a bit bloody serious. A jabbing. A stabbing, even. I shouldn't want him to – ow! – think it's that major. I shouldn't want to encourage him to start poking about with a probe. I shouldn't want him to do that thing they do with the little hammer. Look up 'probe'.."

"*Sonde*," she said, after a bit. "Or *stylet*."

"I wonder which?" I said. A tiny electric shock arced across the tooth in question. "I shall probably try both. *S'il vous plaît m'sieur le dentiste, pas de sonde ou de stylet*."

"*Ou petit marteau?*"

"What?"

"Little hammer."

"Oh, right. *Et pas de petit bloody marteau, either*. How does that sound?"

"Mad," she replied, sympathetically. "You cannot walk into his surgery and start laying down dental procedures. He'll know what to do, if he's any good."

"If," I cried, "if! He could be a bloody butcher. They could all be bloody butchers. Who can guess what dental standards are like in France? Remember when I broke my thumb in, where was it, Poitiers? They just rammed in a suppository the size of a walnut and said don't wiggle it for a month. The French may very well have vastly different pain thresholds from us."

"Everybody," she said, "has a vastly different pain threshold from you."

"I just happen to have particularly sensitive teeth," I said.

Unquestionably, I had one particularly sensitive tooth. It had made this known to me, last midnight, here in Vence, some 900 miles from 12 Upper Wimpole Street, the emollient premises of the world's most understanding dentist, a chap so assiduously trained by me over the long nervous years that I now have enough confidence, when walking in, to take off my hat without an anaesthetic. He was not here. We were here, in this café, this morning, with this dictionary, and, across the square, the sun-winking plates of three alien tooth-jockeys. To whom should I turn?

138

"Look up 'painless'," I said.

"*Sans douleur*," she read, aloud.

"Doesn't sound right," I said. "*Bonjour, êtes-vous un dentiste sans douleur?* It sounds as though I'm inquiring into his personal life. Tell you what, look up 'high-speed drill'."

"You plan to ask him if he uses a – hang on – *un fraisage de grande vitesse?*"

"It would at least be some indication that he kept abreast of things. It wouldn't surprise me if some of these buggers used a brace and bit. Chloroform, possibly. If you were lucky."

She looked at me briefly; then away, to the doorways opposite.

"Personally," she said, "I'd pick the one with the Mercedes."

"Means nothing at all," I said. "Could well be a charlatan. Could well have paid for it out of totally unnecessary bridgework. You'd go in with a twinge, he'd slip you the chloroform, by the time you woke up you'd have a 22-carat lower jaw and he'd be out shopping for a Ferrari."

"Tell him *pas de travail de pont*," she said.

"I don't think you're taking this seriously," I said. "As a matter of fact, I've been wondering whether we ought to settle for Vence at all. Little town like this, what kind of dentists would it attract? Why don't we drive to Antibes? It wouldn't surprise me if Antibes has the most demanding clientele in the world. Or what about Monaco? You can't tell me Rainier lets any old quack bang away with a little hammer."

"True," she said, "and don't forget St Tropez. Bardot's smile, as I understand it, has lost none of its radiance with the passing years."

I finished my coffee. It was no longer hot, but the tooth twanged.

"Alternatively," I said, "I could be in Wimpole Street in three hours."

"Just when I've found out that the word we're after is *poltron?*" she said.

139

I Say, Waiter, This Broth's Spoilt!

Back home after a week of truffling, literally, in the Gallic fleshpots, and therefore seeking some means of retaining the reader's goodwill against the spirit-plummeting prospect of yet another hack banging on about major hot dinners of our time, let me immediately reassure you. This piece is not about food, it is about chefs; it seeks not to praise, but to grumble; and it is motivated not by self-indulgence but by reformist zeal. Especially as the old bad custom in France stands poised to become the new bad custom in Britain, this being the downside of that upside which over the past few years has been bringing us better and better domestic cooking by more and more chefs enjoying the heroic status which the culture increasingly bestows.

Make no mistake, here: I unreservedly accept the great cook as an artist. The bloke who looks at a dead fish and a handful of weeds and discerns within them *rouget à la nage au basilic* is as deserving of that trade description as the one who juggles 26 letters until they have formed *Paradise Lost*, or winkles the Bach Double Violin Concerto out of eight lengths of catgut. I should happily endorse a Nobel Prize for Patisserie, or a Cooks' Corner in Westminster Abbey, and if Her Majesty were to take it in mind to drop the sabre upon some culinary shoulder, I would not stand in her way. For great chefs deserve all the admiration and gratitude a stomach has to give.

140

I ask only that they don't come out seeking it. Cooks should stay in kitchens.

Let us suppose I am happily immersed in a novel; I do not expect the doorbell to ring halfway through, and to find Kingsley Amis standing on the mat, notionally inquiring whether everything is all right, but actually asking me to fall and kiss the hem of his smock. If I am lolling on the South Bank, eyes closed to appreciate the magic fingers plucking the Waldstein from the keyboard, I do not expect to have those eyes snapped open by Alfred Brendel suddenly bellowing: "Well, what do you think of it so far?"

Shift the locale to many a major restaurant, however, and we may stop supposing. Of the four such in which I last week tied on the eager bib, all were culpable, and none more irritatingly so than the one which was the most major of all. Indeed, there are those who would argue that the Ousteau de Baumanière is among the best half-dozen in the world: with its three Michelin stars, five crossed forks and spoons, gules rampant, and countless other ribbons, rosettes, and accolades, it is, given the recent passing of President Ceausescu, possibly the most decorated thing there now is. Nor are the gongs unearned; three stars are translated by the great tyre gourmands as "worth a special journey", but I have little doubt that if there were a fourth star indicating "situated atop the Eiger but well worth approaching by the North Face", the Ousteau would get it.

I had, accordingly, been salivating at its prospect for years, and in the event, not a drop proved to have sprung in vain. We rolled our eyes over the *ravioli de truffes au poireaux*, we caught our breath at the *filets de loup à la vapeur au jus de betterave* – but then, just as we were about to raise the trembling cutlery over the *noisettes d'agneau Baumanière*, the corner of my eye picked up what it most dreaded. A flash of white, no bigger than a man's toque.

The premises freeze-framed, and a susurration rippled through the serried diners. Old M Thuilier had appeared. Untucketed, perhaps, untrumpeted, uncannoned, but even so you never saw such a coming. As table after table paused in sequence and went into an elaborate routine of fawning, and grinning, and gasping, it was as if a ward-round had been crossed with a Mexican wave.

In the 30 minutes he took to reach us, the *noisettes* disappeared, but I cannot remember eating them, so preoccupied was I in composing something gushing to lay at M Thuilier's feet in order that he should not feel we were unworthy to have a couple of hundred quid taken off us. Eventually, he hove to, I gurgled, he nodded, and moved imperiously on. "I didn't catch any of that," said my wife. "Did you say *Please sir, can I have some more*?"

I shall write to Michelin. The time has come for a new little symbol. A toque with three vertical bars in front of it, indicating a restaurant where the chef doesn't appear.

Parts of One Stupendous Hole

Almost everything that there is in the world is in Hayes.

I know what you are going to say, and I advise against it. There will be those of you, I know, who have recently visited the Taj Mahal, say, or the Eiffel Tower, or Harry's Bar, and who are even now hopping about in eagerness to tell me that it is not Hayes you have just got back from, but I enjoin you not to risk making fools of yourselves. I do not say that Agra, or Paris, or Venice do not sport such items, simply that they are also to be found in Hayes. If you know where to look.

I must also stress that they do not exist as entities. Only as components. Millions of them, flat-packed, wrapped in polythene, computer-docketed, bar-coded and neatly shelved; though also, less happily, widely dispersed. The thermostat for the oven in Harry's Bar, for example, may be miles from the wing-nuts necessary for stopping Harry's Bar's letter-box from falling into the Adriatic; nor should you expect the Taj Mahal fusebox to be as near as logic would dictate to the timing device which ensures that the floodlights switch on every night at 7pm, because it could just as well be on the shelf immediately beneath the one which carries the cogs from the Eiffel Tower's winchgear. But they will all be somewhere in Hayes. Given time, you could return from Hayes with the wherewithal to erect the Eiffel Tower in your back garden.

Not, however much I admire it, that I look forward to my annual visit to Hayes. That is why it is an annual visit. During the year, bits conk out, drop off, rot away, and at the end of the long chains of telephone calls and letters and faxes to manufacturers and distributors and service managers, lies – invariably – Hayes. It is the spares capital of the world. You always have to go to Hayes to get the part. But you cannot keep on going to Hayes, because it is a terrible journey, and so you store up your needs, you pile the busted junk in a stair-cupboard until that day when the stair-cupboard is full and there is nothing for it but to load the junk into the car and set off for Hayes.

It is not a terrible journey to get there, mind; you simply follow the Uxbridge Road. It is a terrible journey once you have arrived. For Hayes is not so much amorphous as amoeboid; not only does it expand exponentially year on year, as more and more labour-saving devices come on to the market and immediately start falling apart, it also changes shape inside itself. Every year you go back to where you went the year before, and it has gone somewhere else. There are virtually no roads any more, they have all been replaced by things called Parks and Units and Complexes, and these both mushroom and shuffle about so fast that gazetteers have long since chucked in the cartographical

143

sponge. You might as well carry the Mappa Mundi as the A–Z.

The stranger relies on two things. The first is the goodwill of the locals, most of whom, thank God, speak fluent Sparepart. On this year's trip, last Tuesday, I was carrying an Akai turntable, a Bosch freezer-door and a Neff hob, all to be waved at people in different Complex Unit Parks. Hardly had I crossed the border into the post-modernist Legoland that is Hayes '89 than I was hopelessly lost. I drew up beside two venerable dog-walking Hayesonians.

"Do you know where Bosch is?" I said.

"I think you'll find it near Poggenpohl, now," said the man, "won't he?"

"Between Poggenpohl and Franke," said his wife, firmly.

"Would that be far from Neff?" I said.

"Neff," said the wife, "Neff, now I've seen Neff, haven't I, I've seen Neff just the other side of, was it Zanussi?"

"Zanussi's moved," said her husband. "It's gone behind Miele. I think Neff's just this side of Gaggenau. Your best bet is to ask at The Grapes."

I knew that. The Grapes is always the best bet. The Grapes is the other thing the stranger relies upon. The Grapes is the one fixed point in the mutant world of Hayes. You can always find The Grapes, if only from the crowd of wretched vagrants filing in beneath their burdens of inert microwaves, camcorder fragments and knobless food-mixers.

They knew where Neff was, in The Grapes. They thought, though, that Akai had moved to Hillingdon. So I asked where Hillingdon was, and they said, well, it's Hayes, really, these days.

Caught on the Hop

You will not, looking back, believe how much you learned this morning. As William Butler Yeats all but put it, when you are old and gray and full of sleep, and nodding by the fire, take down this book, and slowly read, and the recollection will knock your nightcap off.

Take the word *euphorbiaceous*. Do not kid me you have heard it before. For you it is entirely new. You have no idea what it means. Nevertheless, you rather like the sound of it. Is it not radiant? Is it not fragrant? Does it not, indeed, exude the very euphony with which its apparent etymology associates it? I know that smiling prefix, you murmur, I know that *eu-*, and if it's good enough for the Greeks, it's good enough for me.

Ha, ha. The Middle English *euphorbia* from which it derives was originally spelt *euphorbea*, because it was not Greek at all but Latin, and spelt that way by Pliny the Elder (AD 23–79), almost certainly to impress his newly adopted son, Pliny the Younger (62-*c* 114). Who, like you, had never heard of Euphorbus. Amazing, now, to think that little Pliny did not know that Euphorbus was the court physician to Juba II, king of Mauretania, but there you are, it's a funny old world. As a matter of fact, I didn't know he was either, until one of my pets ran away. More accurately, jumped away, but I shall come to that later.

First things first. There would be no point going on at all,

145

if you were not to be told that the king of Mauretania was so impressed with his GP that he named a plant after him, which Middle Englishmen decided to spell *euphorbia*. We can be quite frighteningly nationalistic when it comes to loan-words: I once saw *gatto* written on a cakeshop window in Stanmore.

More to the point, take *spurge*. *Spurge* is how Middle Englishmen transculturized the French *espurge* making it a fine, almost exemplary, English word for cleansing the body of impurities. You can hear Middle Englishmen using it, can you not, rural quacks closing the door upon some groaning bedchamber and telling the goodwife, "Im'll be roight as rain, now oi've a-spurged 'im." And let me say, before you begin throwing things, that this is no mere digression. For spurge itself – the item used for spurging – is a plant of the genus *euphorbia*! Its fruit contains an acrid milky juice possessing medicinal properties, some of which clearly did Juba II of Mauretania no end of good, otherwise Dr Euphorbus would have been out on his ear sharpish, and I should today be inconsolably glum over the likely fate of Harry Wharton, my Mexican jumping-bean.

Harry Wharton came into my life on Christmas morning, courtesy of my daughter. He came in a little glass phial, along with Bob Cherry, Johnny Bull, Frank Nugent, and Hurree Jamset Ram Singh. I shook them out on to the breakfast table, and was about to eat them when Harry Wharton, the largest, began rolling around. As I watched, the rest began rolling around, too. Quite uncanny, and slightly pitiful, for a most bizarre reason: my maternal grandfather had been, in his youth, a pavement escape-artist of no talent whatever, and had finally given up struggling to get out of sacks in the Mile End Road in order to be a hardly more successful barber; and, watching these five beans now, I could not forbear the poignant recollection of his failure.

I put them in a bowl, and they continued to hop about so merrily that I had no qualms about leaving them when I went to France on December 28. When I came back last Monday, there were only four there. The largest, Harry

Wharton, had gone. I searched the room, but there was no trace. Distraught – I saw it blindly hopping about Cricklewood, trying, like a peculiar hybrid of Lassie and my grandfather, to get back to Acapulco – I began that chain of inquiry whose fruits lie strewn above.

I learned that the Mexican bean grows on euphorbiaceous plants, and jumps only because concealed within it is the larva of a tortricid moth (L *tortrix* = twister), which writhes more frantically the closer it comes to maturity. Harry Wharton, the Royal Entomological Society concluded, has in all probability lurched from his bowl and burst from his bean. He has become a Cricklewood Jumping Moth.

Relief, then; but fresh anxieties, too: could he survive, without his natural habitat? Relax, said Kew, England is full of spurge.

Drawn, Unhung and Quarterless

It may not make more than a footnote, nor much of a footnote at that, but when the history of these remarkable times comes to be written, my name could well find itself being bandied about.

Let us imagine we are eagerly gobbling our way through the forthcoming Volume XI of *The Oxford History of Soviet Post-Imperialism*. On page 932, there is a Polaroid photograph. Its caption reads:

"Prokurator-Elekt Tadeusz Wojcik (*left*) and soon-to-be Lodz Tram Supremo Miroslaw Orzechowski, seen here enjoying a joke on December 17, 1989. The portrait Wojcik is pointing at is believed to be of Allen Coran, an unknown Englishman."

Only a guess, of course. But on the three or four occasions that I have sidled into the bar of the Polish Club in Princes Gate to stare at myself with, presumably, the same mad eyes that stare back at me from the wall, expatriates have been gathered in the vicinity of my picture in excited knots, jabbering Slavonically with – given the momentous doings in their beloved homeland – understandable vehemence; and on at least two of those occasions, having their snapshots taken. Since almost everyone I have met in the Polish Club has also vowed to hurtle back home at the earliest opportunity and get stuck in to realizing the dreams of 40 years, i.e. becoming a big shot in the New Order, I can only conclude that my own small part in Eastern Europe's extraordinary metamorphosis lies well-enshrined.

It couldn't go on, of course. They needed the wall. They did not tell me why they needed the wall, and I did not like to ask, because one of the answers might be to the effect that when you are re-Balkanizing Europe, you need every square inch of wall-space you can lay your hands on for maps, also big boxes of little coloured flags and a couple of gross of magnetized tanks; or, in the case of Poland, magnetized cavalry.

Anyway, they phoned me last week and said could I pop down to Princes Gate and collect my portrait. Since readers already know why it was hanging there in the first place (see page 75), I shall not bother to explain that it was painted by the ravishing Basha Kaczmarowska, whom I mistakenly, last September, thought was inviting me up to her studio not to see her etchings, but who was in fact frantically trawling sitters for her upcoming exhibition and needed something bald and jowl-hung to make up the set. That is how I wound up leering from a nail in the Polish Club.

Where I should have stayed, even if only in the cellar. For as soon as I put my key in the door and the portrait down in the hall, I knew that I had no idea where to hang it. It is life-size, it dominates. Wherever I put it in the house, it

148

would be making a statement. All of those statements would invite speculation of the highest order, and derision of the lowest. You cannot hang a life-size simulacrum of yourself in the hall, because it says *Welcome to Megalomania Towers*; you cannot hang it in the living-room, because it says *Hallo, I Am A Conversation Piece, Would You Like To Say Something About Me?*; you cannot hang it in the dining room, because it says *Have You Noticed How My Eyes Follow You Round The Soup?*; you cannot hang it in the bedroom, because she says *There's Nothing Going On Between You And This Polish Bimbo, Is There?*

I spent most of the weekend creeping into rooms, locking the door, hammering in hooks as softly as I could, hanging the painting, standing back, taking it down, pliering the hooks out as softly as I could, unlocking the door, and creeping out again.

For the plain fact is that the hanging of a portrait suggests an act of reverence on someone's part, and if that someone is oneself, there are, obviously, more kicks than ha'pence in it. You need a sign underneath informing the gawper that this portrait has been paid for by voluntary subscription raised by loyal troopers of the 17th/21st Uhlans, or hon. members of the Amalgamated Union of Cobblers, or the grateful boys of St Snottie's.

Unable to front up any of those, I can see only one solution. First thing tomorrow, I shall find a brass engraver to run up *Removed From The Polish Club By Democratic Decision*. If nothing else, it catches the spirit of the times.

FEBRUARY

Snappy Dresser

I f you think being a kept man is all beer and skittles, then you have never had two people fiddling with your trousers in a public place, while all the world wondered.

It was not a good weekend at all. To give you some idea of how good it wasn't, I should tell you that if I did not, this Monday afternoon, have certain obligations, e.g. binmen coming tomorrow, car booked in for new brakepads on Thursday, I should even now be lying beneath the plastic surgeon's dissembling scalpel, clutching the one-way ticket to Paraguay which would give me at least an outside chance of starting a new life beyond the derision of my native sod.

You toy with television at your peril. If the trauma of the past few days has taught me nothing else, it has taught me that. As a matter of fact, it has taught me several things else – did you know that it is possible to achieve a lower register than Chaliapin, provided you are prepared to run the risk of detaching your retinas? – but since I intend none of them ever to stand me in any stead whatsoever, they are lessons I shall file and forget.

If you are with me so far, you will have twigged that I

recently signed a contract to appear in a forthcoming television series – let us call it *Scraping The Barrel* – and that one of the requirements (the misguided call them perks) of such foolhardiness is that you get new clothes. If it is a longish series, you get quite a lot of new clothes, because for some reason producers think that if their screenfodder appears in the same shirt two weeks running then mobs of enraged viewers will gather in the car park and begin chucking lumps of dismembered Porsche through the studio windows. The logic which correlates variety of necktie with success of programme escapes me, but it may possibly explain why John Logie Baird, never a natty dresser, died broke.

Now, in the past, I have, when the Devil beckoned, been left to choose my own toilette, and have generally gone for one of the quieter shades of grey, since in the kind of broadcasts I do, the trick is to strive for unobtrusiveness. This time, however, I was told that I should have a dresser. He would pick me up on Saturday morning, and we should trawl the shops together under the guidance of his professional eye.

Guy duly materialized. A charming bloke, if a little flamboyantly shrill for the early hour, and interestingly turned out in piebald buckskins which, I discovered, he runs up himself. He was carrying a little cardboard model of the set which I was to front, and indeed, a little cardboard model of me, in an emerald jacket. Guy, who is after all paid to be sensitive, caught my shudder.

"Yes," he said, "it is a tiny bit whoopsy. But I do think we want to make something of a splash, don't you? I mean, it isn't *Panorama.*"

It was a long day, Saturday. Did you see me in Austin Reed? I was the one in the red velvet blouson, shrinking behind a trouser-rack while Guy cried at the assistant, "No, no, no, he's much too bonny for scarlet!"

Did you see me in Cecil Gee? I was the one in the green plaid waistcoat trying to pass himself off as a dummy while Guy cried "Can you wave your hands about, love? Can you

154

give something?" Did you see me in Simpson's? I was the one in the ivory seersucker, vainly struggling to look more seer and less sucker while Guy and his new friend the floorwalker went into hysterical convulsions about my backside.

And almost the worst of all was that Guy resolutely refused to divulge our relationship. "Tell them it's for telly, and they come over all of a doodah," he explained. "Let them think we're just buddy-buying."

I stared at him. He gave me a little shove. This was in Harrod's.

And the worst of all? The worst of all was that Guy was carrying a big bag of notes. Every time he said, "Yes, he looks lovely, I'll take it," he snapped open the bag, and peeled the wad. I stood by the till, jutting my jaw rhomboid and gravelling my voice till the windows rattled.

Selfish, really. For when, exhausted, we closed the nightmare in a pub and I came clean on my discomfort, Guy put down his gin and said: "Yes, well, and what about *my* image?"

And I said: "What about your image?"

And Guy said: "Well, you're hardly Lord Alfred, love."

Have I Skipped Anything?

I may be all right. I may get away with it. What I have done is, I have put Little Black Sambo in the armoured personnel carrier and I have wrapped 8ft of blue cord carpet round it and I have put the whole thing in the space where the bathroom cabinet with the duff door was before I took it out and shoved it into the cavity formerly occupied by my late father-in-law's old Ferguson. What I have done with my late father-in-law's old Ferguson is carry it upstairs again. I feel a lot better now. I was very uneasy carrying it downstairs in the first place, because I have seen old Fergusons in the Portobello Road and they can fetch serious money if they are in mint condition, and my late father-in-law's will be in mint condition as soon as I can track down a Bakelite knob, which I have been planning to do ever since he became late, in 1981. When it has a Bakelite knob on it, you will be able to turn the dial and get Hilversum and Allouis and Daventry.

I see I have not explained about getting away with it. What I am trying to get away with is not giving the impression that I have brought my children up as war-mongering racists, and I shall be able to do that provided someone is not after 8ft of blue cord carpet. If they grab the blue cord carpet, Little Black Sambo and the Action Man armoured personnel carrier will fall out. It will not be quite so bad if they are after 12ft of old gold Axminster; if they are after 12ft of old gold Axminster, the only thing that will fall out will be the 1979 Wrexham football team, a ballcock, and a headless golliwog, and I can probably get away with this on the grounds that now his head has gone, you cannot tell he was a golliwog, a lot of toys wear white gloves, probably. That my son and I once supported Wrexham to the extent of painting our Subbuteo team red-and-black, I can live with: the cackling which that support would now invite is probably no worse than, say, the accompaniment to an exposed ballcock.

All this fretting is down to Mr Coombs. I cannot expect you to recall that Mr Coombs was the one looking down through the hole after my roof blew off. I know you have a lot on your minds, but this is the same Mr Coombs. He finished the new roof on Tuesday, and his parting words were: "I'll ring CPL about the wossname, skip, and they'll collect it, but as it's only half full, you may want to chuck

156

some stuff on, so I'll give you a day, right?" And I thought, this is a golden opportunity, I have been meaning to clear the loft for 18 years, and that was Tuesday taken care of, 14 times up and 14 times down, and a fair amount of jetsam making return journeys.

Like the toasters. When I first brought the box of toasters down, there was a man on the pavement sitting in a busted ladderback chair, and he said "Not a bad chair, this, just needs a couple of stretchers", and I said "Take it" and he said "You want them toasters?" which was enough to give me second thoughts, because I have always known in my heart of hearts that you could get toasters repaired, so I took them up to the loft again, but by mid-afternoon I had third thoughts, and they came down once more, wrapped in 10ft of burgundy Wilton this time, because I didn't want the bloke coming past again and wondering why I would rather throw them away than give them to him.

The collected works of Enid Blyton went back up on the ninth trip. I carried them balanced on the wooden lavatory seat, because I had my flared dress-trousers in my other hand, draped over the busted pogo-stick. That was because when I came down on the eighth trip with the fan heater that neither fans nor heats, I looked at the top-dressing on the skip and suddenly saw myself as others might see me: a pitiful wretch in an ancient tuxedo, hopping home to his clapped-out lavatory and the unfortunate children he was raising on a diet of Noddy, war and fourth-division football.

For what is a loft-filled skip but a three-dimensional family album? And who in his right mind would lay 20 years of his life beside the kerb to implore the passing tribute of a sneer? In fact, staring out, now, at what seems to be only a pile of old carpet, I am beginning to wonder about even that. Do I really want the world to know that we were once caught up in the fashion for mushroom shagpile?

I have an hour or so before CPL turns up. All I have to do is clear a space in the loft.

Lay That Pistol Down

I*t is with a tremulous heart and no less unsteady hand that I set pen to paper in this year of grace 19-, for no more honourable a reason than to unburden myself to you, dear reader, of that dreadful catalogue of events which only your gentle and indulgent spirit . . .*

Born a century too late, is the problem. A hundred years ago, and I should have been able to hurl myself into this *feuilleton* with the only style befitting its bizarre and fathomless matter. I might even have got away with declaiming that it was my belief, founded upon my experience, that the lowest and vilest alleys of London did not present a more dreadful record of sin than did the smiling and beautiful countryside, especially since countryside was what Cricklewood then was, a fair clop from Baker Street but well worth the hansom fare if you were a beaky violinist with a penchant for the insoluble.

As it is, I shall just have to lay the facts before you in the mundane literary fashion of the times, and leave the Victorian sinisterness of those facts to glimmer through as best it can.

A couple of weeks ago, I drove to Riverside Nurseries to buy a horse-chestnut tree. Purists may say that I should have poked a conker in and taken my chances, but if they do it will be because they are young purists, unable to appreciate that when a gardener reaches a certain age, he cannot muck

158

about with seeds if he hopes to realize a dream of sitting beneath something spreading.

Within the hour, I was driving back with the hood down and the tree strapped into the seat beside me and draped over the back with its top-gallant tracery whistling in the wind, for all the world like Isadora Duncan. But even taller: twelve feet of tree this was, and guaranteed to enconker before too many of my remaining autumns had dwindled.

It will be appreciated from this that what it needed was a big hole; the day was mild, and the soil yielding, and I was soon lustily swinging the spade among the importunate robins and congratulating myself for doing my small bit towards making up for all the luckless trees that have been chopped down over the past 30 years so that I could earn my living. You may thus gather that I was in pretty high spirits; and they lasted right to the bottom of the hole.

I was three feet down, about to cast the spade aside and reach for the bonemeal, when I struck metal. I peered in, suddenly fearful of power conduit or sewerman's helmet, but saw, with relief, that it was only a small earthy lump of something. I reached down, and brought it up. It weighed a couple of pounds, and it was shapeless; until I poked the mud off. When I poked the mud off, it became a revolver.

The afternoon suddenly grew slightly less mild, at least on the back of the neck. I left the tree, and went into the house, and ran the gun under the tap until the rest of the mud was gone. It was remarkably rustless, possibly because it seemed to have been plated, possibly because of the few shards of paper which had come away under the tap and which may have been the remains of some more substantial wrapping. Not that this mattered any more than the fact that it could, clearly, no longer be fired; what mattered was that it could equally clearly have been fired once, and that it had not buried itself.

There are not many reasons for burying a revolver, especially in a domestic garden. My wife suggested I take it to the police, but I held back, partly because I didn't want them storming in with labradors called Radar and digging up the lawn in the hope of finding what might have once been on the wrong end of the gun, but mainly because the gun had been buried a long time ago, and the chances of their finding whoever might have done what might have been done were remote enough for me to prefer them to get on with collaring the ratbag who nicked my car radio in 1983. I know it was buried a long time ago, because the gun-dealer I did take it to put its interment at around 1900, give or take. It had, he said, been made about 1860.

Quite what happened on my premises some time between 1860 and 1900 I have, a fortnight on, almost stopped thinking about.

Roses Are Blooming in Cricklewood

S hort of actually spotting the lark on the wing and the snail on the thorn, there is nothing so sets a Cricklewood villager up of a morning than the horse on the tarmac.

It usually happens around 11am, that singular moment of the suburban day when the palpable calm which suddenly drops on residential short-cuts after the last company Sierra has slewed through its imagined chicane is, in its turn, gently broken by the small sounds and movements of peripolitan life.

The 1930s return to the suburbs they bore: women with unraised consciousness clop carefully down crazy-paving paths, click wrought-iron gates discreetly, and clop up the paths next door for milky Nescafé and rich tea Osbornes and anecdotes of salon and school rota; elderly gentlemen in corduroy trilbies tug terriers away from trees and site them civic-mindedly in gutters; a milk-float brakes, rattling, to allow a householder with a pint of gold-top to swap it for a pint of skimmed, and her echoing laugh panics the black-birds under the privets; a window-cleaner, snapping his leather, struts his stuff with that special strut which bespeaks lecherous fictions, a sort of walking wink; a daily polishes a bell-push furiously, and "Volare" chimes and chimes. Milly-Molly-Mandy lives, and William Brown, and Mrs Dale.

And, after a bit, you hear a hoof, and the snort of a substantial nostril, and you go to your window for a sly suburban shufti through your curtains, and riding by is what can only be called a constable. It is not filth, nor fuzz nor the Old Bill; it is not a pig. It is *comes stabuli*, the count of the stable. It is the apotheosis of suburban order.

It does not matter that the long fetlock of the law is very possibly the least useful instrument in the maintenance of that order. Cricklewood neither goes in for riots, nor often requires a *cordon chevalier* for mounted royals. A number of cars get nicked, much graffiti is sprayed on walls, video-recorders visible through unlocked windows tend to change owners fairly crisply, but these are not situations for which a baton charge is the textbook answer. True, domestic alarms go off with enough regularity to suggest that Cricklewood is in a permanent state of forced entry, but even if 99.7 per cent of these were not down to iffy wiring, sudden breezes, and the cat getting up in the middle of the night for a cheese sandwich, the last thing most householders would want is a bloke galloping upstairs on a big chestnut gelding to check for boots sticking out from under the curtains.

No, the mounted policeman is not about the practical application of the law, he is principally there, at least from the consumer's point of view, in order to suggest that he does not need to be there at all. Here is Cricklewood, his immaculately curried horse announces, here is Cricklewood,

161

his shimmering accoutrements confirm, where life is so lawful and so ordered that all that is called for is ceremonial patrol. He is not so much for the suburb, as of it.

And what could bond him more tightly to this emollient suburban scenario than this morning's incident?

A couple of hours ago, I was shoulder-deep in the gully beside my garage, happily reaming a drain, when the horse came by. I stood up, because ceremony should be a two-way trade, and bade good morning to the constable. He reined in.

"Looks like we've seen the back of the rain," he said.

"And the wind's dropped," I pointed out, expertly.

The horse lifted its tail.

"Well, must get on," said the constable, after a bit.

To his credit, he did not refer to what had happened astern. He simply touched his peak, and I nodded, because that is all that Cricklewood protocols required. After he had gone, I went into the garage to get a shovel. The last time I did that was 40 years ago. You got threepence for it, then, from Mr Creswell at Number 7. I have my own roses, now.

When I came out of the garage, a neighbour was standing by the gift, with her own shovel.

"Ah," she said.

"No, no," I said. "We'll go halves."

Suburbia could offer no more quintessential moment. As I stooped, a burglar alarm went off, somewhere; but the horse, at the corner now, did not even break into a trot.

Feels Natural

It may be counted a major stroke of good fortune that, on Wednesday, the Princess of Wales poked her hand through the right hole: "DI GRABS JEW'S EAR!" is not a headline one would care to see exciting the world's wire services.

In the event, what the radiant fingers groped for, clasped, and indeed correctly identified unseen, was an elephant's molar. I know this, because an hour later I did two-thirds of that myself. I fell only at the final hurdle, but I can live with it: I tell myself that HRH must have felt many an elephant's tooth in her time, all those tropical tours, all those inaugural buns popped in when opening this or that zoological garden, all those chums, doubtless, with backyard enclosures of their own, the soft Hampshire evenings echoing to the trumpeting of pachyderm and scion alike as the tuxedoed guests strolled among the rhododendrons and shot the breeze.

She and I arrived at the tooth in question by reaching through one of the apertures offered by the Feely Box. The Feely Box is in the new Activity Centre of the Natural History Museum, and it was particularly fitting that the Princess should be there to open it just as her husband, across at Kew, had finished berating the earth's despoilers for the destruction of the rainforests. For, increasingly, the mission of both institutions is to concern themselves with the conservation of what is, in order to avoid becoming the repositories of what was, and it was pleasing to find future monarchs severally addressing themselves simultaneously to the flora and fauna they hope notionally to inherit.

Inheritance, in fact, is now the theme of the NHM, embodied in a resonant quotation which hangs on its wall to remind us that "we do not inherit the earth from our parents, we borrow it from our children"; and it was therefore particularly reassuring not only to find the NHM teeming with my tiny creditors, but to find them interacting so enthusiastically with the exhibits which the new enlightened NHM policy encourages them to muck about with. *Please Touch!* is the campaign anthem, which only goes to show that a lifetime spent in considering what made a dinosaur tick does not necessarily disqualify a person from understanding the nature of somewhat younger organisms.

Please stick head in scorpion's pincers! was how Brendan interpreted the rubric. I found Brendan in the Creepie Crawlie Gallery, a spot I had previously visited only in nightmares. The scorpion was 10ft long. Confronted with a similar item in the Odeons of my own youth, a man called Chuck would have cried, "Stand back, Professor, there's only one language these things understand!" and emptied his carbine to no effect whatever, but we have come a long way since then.

"It holds you like this," explained Brendan. He closed the scorpion's claw over his head. "Then it brings its tail over and stings you. Then it drags you up there to its jaws, and chews you to little bits."

"It's got an exoskeleton," said the little girl next to Brendan. "I've built one. It cost £4.95."

"I've built a stegosaurus," said another girl, muscling in the way kids do. "And I've just bought a triceratops to go with it." She waved the bag from the NHM shop. "I think they ought to do radio-controlled ones. You could have a swamp, and they could all walk about in it."

"I bought a mammoth," said an extremely tiny boy. "Look."

"You don't have to build *that*!" cried the second girl. "You just blow it up. It's not a model. It's a balloon, is what that is."

"Did you know," said Brendan, who had come out of the

164

scorpion, "that half of all the species in the world are beetles?"

"I've got a stag-beetle at home," said another boy. "It's that long."

"I've stroked a tarantula," said the first girl. "At Syon Park. They let you. This man had it walking up his arm, and I stroked it."

Astonishing. My credo has ever been, if it's too big to step on, run away. What's happened to kids? Where are their phobias? Shamed, I went back to the Feely Box, just to show I was a brave little soldier, and when I stuck my hand in, it touched something unsavoury. I drew it out again, quickly.

"Bracket's fungus," explained the attendant. "Also known as Jew's Ear. But we've stopped calling it that, of course."

Quite. All part of the learning process.

Mint Condition

It's an odd feeling to know what you'll be sucking when you're 87.

It is both locally odd – how will this tongue feel, then, will it have shrivelled and lost sensation, will it be lolling from side to side, will it be jabbering to itself? How will these teeth feel, will they wobble, will they clack, will they be there at all or have given gummy way to shimmering prostheses? What about these lips, will they be vacantly grinning, crabbily denouncing, lecherously puckering, will

165

they perhaps, as they suck, be attempting simultaneously to whistle a fetching track from 83-year-old Paul McCartney's 233rd golden album?

– and less locally odd, which is to say, where will this sucking head *be*, provided it is not six feet under something? Will it be staring glumly from the barred window of the Bide-A-Wee Sunset Scrapyard? Floating happily on some sunsoaked Martian canal, courtesy of Cook's Interplanetary Winter Breaks? Craning for a glimpse of the scampered single which will thwart Latvia of England's follow-on? Thronging loyally in Downing Street, to express its personal good wishes to its Prime Minister on the occasion of her 100th birthday?

Indeed, might this head, wherever it is, be wondering nervously whether its recent run-of-the-mill transplant means that it has acquired a new body, or that the body has acquired a new head, and what the answer implies *vis-à-vis* its pension entitlements?

We can confidently – and perhaps fortunately – answer none of this. The future is a foreign country, they will do things differently there. All we can be sure of is what the head will be sucking, in 2026; if it is sucking anything it will be sucking a Trebor Extra Strong Mint.

We know this because of the generosity of Mr Roger Munby. And the possibility that that generosity may contain an element of shrewdness must be allowed to detract not one whit from it, since Mr Munby is Trebor's Executive Director of Marketing, and he would be untrue to his lights – and we should all think the worse of him – if he did not executively direct the market at every conceivable opportunity. And at the odd inconceivable one, too.

In December, you may recall, I abused the reader's hospitality by banging on to the effect that my new navy overcoat had been nicked from a cloakroom peg in the Garrick Club, and I speculated as to the kind of swine who might have pulled such a stroke – because December was in the days before we had heard about Peregrine Worsthorne and the Garrick Mafia, and if I had known then what we all

166

know now, I would have kept my trap shut (indeed, this seems as good a time as any to apologize. Keep the coat, *paysano*, I hope it's nice and warm, and if it isn't roomy enough under the arms to accommodate professional bulges, send the alteration bill to me).

I heard nothing more – you will say luckily – until last week, when a small box, forwarded by *The Times*, arrived at my door. It did not, however, contain an overcoat. It contained 36 rolls of Trebor Extra Strong Mints, and a letter in which, after many a solicitous murmur, Mr Munby concluded: " . . . although I cannot stretch to a replacement cashmere coat, I can at least provide some warming comfort in the deep winter's chill."

How could he have guessed what he had done? It is not his fault – even Wordsworth, than whom no one could have been more of a stranger to executive market-directing, believed the best portions of a good man's life were the little, nameless, unremembered acts of kindness and of love, remaining utterly oblivious to how much they can screw their hapless recipients up.

For I am funny about mints. I suck exactly one tube a year. I know this, because I invariably buy a tube at Christmas, when I tend not only to drink more uninterruptedly than normal, but also to breathe on more people, including policemen, more frequently. By New Year's Day, there are usually two mints left in the packet, which collect fluff for a month or so before getting summarily eaten in a sort of general tidying-up of the pockets.

So when I look, as I look now, at Mr Munby's gift, I see the next 36 years. Let J. Alfred Prufrock measure out his life in coffee-spoons, mints are my meter. One by one, the rolls will go, as Yule follows Yule; and which, I wonder, will run out first, the box or I?

MARCH

Sport of Kings

B etter men than I will get the plums, of course. That is only fair. That is only cricket. You would not expect a lifetime batting average of 4.7 to pull a major monarchy, particularly given that a number of the more impressive scores were made on sand. I recall 38 at Clacton one year, though admittedly that included a chance to the old lady at second slip when I was still in single figures, and if she hadn't been gobbling a choc-ice at the time, history would tell a very different tale.

C. B. Fry's average, you may recall, was standing at 50.22 when they offered him the throne of Albania, including 94 centuries; all, as I understand it, on grass, and most of them while he was concurrently holding not only his place in the England soccer squad but also the world long-jump record. God knows how Zog beat him to throne, probably got so far ahead in the marathon one year that he managed to take 8 for 32 while waiting for the rest of the field to catch up and make a photogenic finish of it. Doubtless went through the tape and carried on running, straight into a world-record pole-vault off his bat.

I see that not all of you do recall the C. B. Fry business, which suggests that you are not presently immersed in *Life Worth Living*, the autobiography in which Fry retails the glorious story. Just after the conclusion of the Great War, Fry trotted off to the Geneva Peace Conference as speech-writer for Ranjitsinhji, a delegate with an average of 56.37 (which presumably explains why he was also the Maharaja of Nawanager). Anyway, during a lull in the international chin-wagging, the Bishop of Albania let it be known that his country was looking not only for a king but for an English sporting gentleman to be that king, especially if he had an income of £10,000 a year, and that the name of C. B. Fry topped his list. Tickled by this, Ranjhi offered to cough up the sinecure if Fry accepted, but Fry hummed and hawed too long, which he seems subsequently to have regretted: "How long I remained a candidate I do not know," he writes, "but Mussolini would not have disposed of me as easily as he disposed of King Zog."

The real point of this captivating gobbet, and the relevant one this morning, is that the Albanians had put Fry's name in the frame for two coincidental reasons: (1) the status of English cricket had never been higher, and (2) the stability of Eastern Europe had never been lower.

If you are not currently absorbed in a choc-ice, there is a drift here which you may have caught. For did that same coincidence not just pop up again and gently loop its way towards second slip? Does there not seem to you to be an answer to the fissiparous hysteria currently racking the fraught territory between the Baltic and the Caspian, and might that answer not lie half a world away, at Sabina Park locale of England's extraordinary triumph over the West Indies?

It might, and some of it might well lie slightly nearer, though, as I adumbrated earlier, the plums will go to better men. For, while this week's resounding endorsement of Mr Gorbachov's reconstituted presidency may mean a slight delay in the establishment of the Gooch Dynasty under Tsar Graham I, I have every confidence that the day cannot be far off when the Warsaw heralds will be bugling the accession of King Lamby, when Archduke Gladstone will be waving to the delirious mobs in Wenceslas Square, and when Crown Prince Wayne and his radiant consort will be riding in state through the cheering streets of Bucharest.

As to the, as it were, minor counties, I cannot guess whom the kingmakers of Estonia or Latvia or Lithuania are currently shortlisting, but I doubt that I am alone in trusting that the spinners will not be left out. Though not, perhaps, a household word where major Balkanologists forgather, I beg leave to suggest that Armenia would benefit hugely from the wisdom, experience, and general dependability which would accompany the founding of the House of Hemmings.

As for me, well, 4.7 and medium-pace daisy-cutters allow one few illusions. I shall have to wait: the new monarchies, once established, will want to re-create the aristocratic infrastructures of yesteryear, and, having popped Fry back on the shelf and taken down *Burke's Royal Families of Europe*, I have little doubt that a cap can be found to fit.

Margrave of Pomerania has a ring to it. If I can remember not to flash at rising balls outside the off-stump, I could be well in, there.

Still Here in Spirit

Last evening, I had an intimation of immortality.
It was not, I'm afraid, *a premier grand cru* intimation, it was not a sight of that immortal sea which brought us hither, it was not even a high instinct

173

before which my mortal nature did tremble like a guilty thing surprised; because in order to experience these, one must, as you know, have a faith that looks through death, and as I have a faith which has its work cut out focusing on next Tuesday, I have long given up the ambition of literal immortality. But that does not mean that I do not hanker, like many of us, after a little nominal imperishability: while I have come reluctantly to accept that when I lie a-mouldering in the grave, nothing will go marching on, I should nevertheless like to fix it for some small remnant to potter about a bit.

There are a few traditional procedures for taking a crack at this, but none comes guaranteed. Contract, for example, something peculiar, and there is just a chance it will get into the textbooks as Coren's Syndrome, chuck yourself off somewhere picturesque and it might thereafter be known as Coren's Leap, strike it lucky with a paper-shop at a major T-junction, then cab-drivers might well continue to refer to it as Koren's Korner long after the moss has obscured your headstone, spend a lifetime in innovative wrestling or cuisine, and you might well leave these professions the richer by a Half-Coren, say, or a Sole Bonne Cricklewood ...but the odds against such coups are unacceptably whim-dependent.

No, stick to your last has ever been my motto, even if the result is doomed to be cobblers; and up until last night, therefore, my bids for immortality had always hung on words. Coin a snappy neologism, catch the eye of the *Oxford English Dictionary*, and I would live forever. The OUP does not strike people off: once in, a word – be it ever so subsequently unused – is there for good.

Every year, therefore, I dangle something in front of them. Twice, I have come close: the first, in 1976, was *wossname*, the second, in 1982, *narmean* – neither one a jewel in the lexical crown perhaps, not a *chortle*, not a *snark*, but items nevertheless that I should be proud to have my name immortally attached to in the *OED* as onlie begetter

174

of. On both occasions, academic inquiries reached me as to their provenance, public appearances, all that; but nothing came of it.

Two Tuesdays ago, in *The Times*, I cast this year's bait. (Still only February, but why hang about? Now that the *OED* is computerized on CD-ROM, updating is a doddle; if you had a VDU, you might see yourself immortalized before you could say Jack Wossname.) My new contender was *peripolitan*, a little corker though I says it as shouldn't, and unquestionably a cultural notch or two up on *narmean*, narmean?

Nothing much happened. A couple of logomachs wrote in, prepared, if I may précis their admiration, to meet me behind the London Library bicycle shed and beat me to a pulp, but from Oxford, nothing. And then, at 6pm yesterday, the phone rang.

I was fixing drinks at the time. My wife was having a kir, I was having a pink vodka, and I had put the ice in both glasses and splashed the cassis in the one and the angostura in the other when she called from the hall that there was someone on the phone from Oxford asking about *peripolitan*. I hurtled; rugs flew. For how could this not be it? *Peripolitan* was the best new word in the world. It had been lying around for 30 centuries, waiting to be coined.

The caller turned out to be some grisly pedant wanting to know what gave me the right, etc. Broken, I shuffled back to the kitchen, sloshed the vodka and the Sancerre into the prepared glasses and passed one to my wife. And she cried: "God almighty!"

I sniffed my own. They really ought to make cassis a different colour from angostura. But then I tasted it; and with it, immortality.

I do not need to find a new word any more. Consider John Collins, potman at Limmer's Hotel, consider Guido Martini, bartender at the Waldorf Astoria, consider James Pimm, oysterateur of Poultry – names now, literally, on every lip.

For vodka with a dash of cassis on the rocks is a very

175

remarkable drink. I urge you to get your teeth around a Bloody Coren tonight. If only to stop him coming up with words like *oysterateur*.

Look At Me When I'm Talking!

The trouble with straws in the wind is that anyone spotting a percentage in gleaning them might well end up with enough to make a brick. And a brick in the wind is, as any metaphorician will tell you, a very different kettle of fish.

As I write this, I have before me a heart-warming photograph of a woman with a telephone in her hand, and a little girl on her knee. The woman is smiling, and the child is waving. An ordinary enough materfamilial vignette you will say, provided you can summon the requisite pomposity, but that is because you do not know the half of it. The half of it is that this winsome snapshot is not ordinary at all; it is, in fact, the photograph of a video-telephone screen, and the other half of it, therefore, is that, somewhere, on another video-telephone screen to which this one is connected, there will be a complementary picture of the smilee/wavee. Probably daddee.

Which suddenly makes it a mite less heart-warming; for something chill has begun to creep up an artery. Not, of course, that Taurus Business Systems of Thurnby think so: Taurus Business Systems of Thurnby believe their video-telephone to be "the most exciting communications device of the 1990s" (a startlingly confident claim, given the infancy

176

and the strong likelihood that well before 1999 the Japanese will have perfected an egg capable of entertaining you with a hologram projection of Hoagy Carmichael singing *Stardust* while you wait for it to boil).

There is, however, no gainsaying Taurus's further claim, likewise taken from the elegant leaflet they sent me as a potential customer, that "communications will never be the same again". In the electronics war, retreat is unknown, and if the video-phone catches on it will never catch off. These days, not only is non-necessity the mother of invention; indispensability is its grandchild. Especially with telephones. You have only to travel Inter-City: the carriage is a horizontal phone booth. Every time the train lurches, 200 people squawk: "Hallo, hallo, are you still there?" A few years ago, this would have been a successful revue song.

A few years ahead, the scenario will be immeasurably ghastlier. Yesterday I rang Taurus – as yet invisibly, so that when the chap said video-phones were really catching on fast, I could not tell whether or not he was looking me square in the eye. But I give him the benefit of the doubt, because I know that my doubt has always ended up as somebody's benefit.

All I have to do is say: "*Desk-top* computers, don't make me laugh!" or "People walking around *with stereos on their heads*, pull this one!" for the Nikkei average to leap 1,000 points.

Thus, though it now costs £994.75 to buy two video-telephones able to transmit talking pictures to each another, and though very few people have them, very soon it will cost £11.99, and everyone will have them.

"Why is this Luddite dingbat railing against so wondrous a boon?" you will even now be crying. "Does he not want to be able to blow kisses at his distant loved ones while he is celebrating the closure of his deal with Happitrash Novelties (Kyoto) Inc?" Well, possibly, depending perhaps on whom I am celebrating it with at the Kyoto end, but are we still so green that we cannot see the iron truth in the velvet marketing? Con the leaflet deeper: "Use this video to see

177

goods for sale, to choose a photographic model for an assignment, or to see new products in three dimensions."

No need, I feel, to dot i's and cross t's, where the conjunction of eyes and tease is only too apparent. The phone rings, unbidden, in 1996, and who is this but a man in a camel-hair coat offering me a double-glazed Skoda loft extension, or a fabulous chance to win a sun-soaked weekend on the Gdansk Riviera? If, that is, it is not ravishing Sharon Chatline murmuring to me from her delightful leatherette boudoir?

Nor is it merely exploitative intrusion we have to fear: the present telephone's infirmity is its greatest boon, it cannot see us when we cover the mouthpiece and concoct excuses, she's not here right now, I have mumps, we're going to be in Mongolia that night, the cheque went off yesterday . . . what will you do in 1996, stick a hand over the lens while you prevaricate and lie?

"The possibilities are endless!" shrieks the Taurus leaflet. Well, yes; and the probabilities?

Fungus the Bogeyman

Up until a year or so ago, I should not have given them a second thought. The first thought would have been ample. The first thought would have been to kick the life out of them. But Jonathon Porritt has changed all that. They are my brothers now. Possibly my dinner. It amounts to the same thing. *Pace* W.H. Auden, we must eat one another or die. One day, after all, they will eat me. They like it around cemeteries.

They also, suddenly, like it around my lawn. I do not know why this should be so when it wasn't before, though I suppose it is the greenhouse effect, because everything else seems to be (I have not the slightest doubt that the recent peculiar events in Eastern Europe will all turn out to be meteorological in origin). They always visited my lawn regularly, mind, but you could tell they didn't like it, because they died, and that is generally a reliable test of whether something likes anything. In fact, you hardly needed boots: in the old days, I would spot them from the window, standing wonkily in little sporadic gangs, thin, pale, sickly, and by the time I had pulled my wellies on for the kicking and run outside, they would have keeled over and withered.

Yesterday I woke early, thanks to the month's third hurricane, and hurtled to the bedroom window to see what had been horizontalized this time. (If this climatic change is permanent, the architecture of England will be compelled to change permanently with it. We shall all have to live in circular bungalows with flat roofs, and no one will be allowed to grow a tree taller than four feet. The only fences you see will be in museums.) Anyway, the garden contained the usual detritus of trellis, tiles, bushes, bin-lids, flower-pots, and other assorted stuff which the night had brought to Cricklewood from Huddersfield and Rhyl – but these were not what trapped the attention. They, after all, were merely scattered across the lawn. They did not cover it.

What covered it was mushrooms.

Not, furthermore, the emaciated specimens of yester-year. These were serious fungi. You could tell that not merely from their size, but from the fact that the gale seemed to be having no effect on them. They did not flinch. They did not snap. When it comes to roofing, I said to myself, the gnomes can teach us a thing or two.

I hurried downstairs and out into the howling dawn, booted, but only against the wet. There would be no kicking today, partly, as I say, because the Earth requires us to be

179

one band of brothers, now, but also because we have learned not to squander her benisons. The mushrooms were no longer a parasite on my lawn, they were a crop on my field. They also, it must be said, pandered to that fantasy of self-sufficiency which has ever tugged the sleeve of urban man: this year mushrooms, next year barley, a pig where the rockery is, perhaps, fruit trees where the inessential roses stand, hens clucking in the toolshed, oysters in the pond . . .

I gazed at the massed ranks of plump stalks and broad caps. Where had they come from? Were they by-blows of restaurant jetsam, typhooned here to burgeon in my greenhoused soil? Were they spores from the Perigord, franchised by the wind to make nonsense of EC controls? Whatever their provenance, you did not have to be a Sainsbury's mycologist to identify some twenty quidsworth of sizzling nutriment.

Always provided – you guessed? – that they were edible. I ran inside again, we had a book somewhere. An hour later, I knew where. I opened *Mushrooms*, *Toadstools and Fungi* by Alan Major. Its first line is "There are some 200,000 species of fungus in the world".

It is four hours later, now: almost lunchtime – or would be, if there were not 200,000 species of fungus in the world. I am standing in the middle of my crop, which, two minutes ago, I finally decided were Fairy Ring Champignons, "much relished by connoisseurs". Joy! Or, rather: joy? For, one minute ago, poised to commence garnering, I turned the page to find a picture of the False Champignon, "thus known because it sometimes appears among edible Fairy Ring Champignons. Poisonous."

And, at a guess, not much relished by connoisseurs. So what do I do now, Jonathon? I mean, friendship of the earth is all very well, but it has to cut both ways.

Unnatural Act

Last Thursday, I made my professional acting debut. I made it at the Cottesloe Theatre, because at my age the trick is to start big. There is no point mucking about in local rep, years of hobbling in and out muttering "There is a young person at the door, madame," and waiting for the chance to play Osrick.

I had not been on a stage for 42 years. 1948 was when I made my amateur debut, in the Mr Hoskyns adaptation of *Hiawatha*. The audition was pretty tough: your mother had to know where to lay her hands on a chicken, no easy task in the Attlee years. What mine could mainly lay her hands on was mince or shin, neither of which made much of a war bonnet. Anyway, she managed to get a little pullet and I managed to get a little role; I had to come on and scan the horizon for the sort of things redskins scan the horizon for, and it was lucky there was only one performance, because stage fright drove the thumb of my scanning hand into my eye and the next day the eye came up like a plum, and had there been a second performance, I should not have been able to go on. There would have had to have been a management announcement that, due to indisposition, the part of Third Brave would be played by David Collingwood, wearing Mrs Coren's pullet.

Given this early trauma it is hardly surprising that I allowed 42 years to go by before taking another crack at the boards, and that when I did go back, it was entirely unintentional. I got to star in *Ma Rainey's Black Bottom* simply by buying a ticket to see it.

The Cottesloe is not so much a theatre in the round as a floor in the round. The stage's perimeter is the first row of seats. Since I had booked by telephone, I did not know that I should be sitting not merely in the first row, but in pole position. I was next to the piano. I was so next to the piano that I could have made a fair fist of Chopsticks without moving from my seat.

The piano is a major component of August Wilson's fine play, which concerns itself with the 1927 recording session at which the great blues singer and her band convened at a Chicago studio to enwax the title masterpiece. You will now understand why the piano is central to the action; you will further understand why, when the house lights dim, the piano is bathed in a big fat spotlight of its own; and if you are truly understanding, you will feel empathetic gooseflesh bubbling for the one member of the audience forced to share that spotlight with the cast.

Even before the play started, stage fright had desiccated my throat and driven its moisture out through either armpit. How my thumb failed to end up in my eye, God alone knows. This was because I often have a problem at the theatre, and as the spotlight warmed my head, the vision came upon me – since I had paid by an identifying credit card – of, at the end, a management announcement to the effect that the part of the Snoring Philistine had been played by Alan Coren.

I thank my lucky stars that the play was so riveting as to save me from at least this embarrassment. I curse, however, my unlucky ones for the text that drove those rivets home: for *Ma Rainey's Black Bottom* derives its conflict from the confrontation between black aspiration and white exploitation. Seven black actors embody the former, three white actors embody the latter. Leaving a fourth white actor (unpaid) trapped between them.

How to react, with 700 spectating eyes on me? A black actor stares into my own from three feet away and delivers a joke simultaneously funny and savage: how much do I laugh, how much do I quail, how far should I manifest my comprehension of the resonances before I blemish the theme of white insensitivity upon which the play depends? When the jazz belts out, is it over the top to tap the spotlit feet in time? When the ravishing Jacqueline de Peza shimmies past, bent on seduction, does the fourth white man look at her with lust or dispassion?

Nearly three hours of this, and I acted my heart out; and I thought I had done all right, until the notices came in. You recall last Thursday? It was the day England beat the West Indies, and joy had betrayed me into childishness. But how could I have known, when I was dressing, what the evening would require of me?

"In my opinion," said my wife's review, "the MCC tie was a mistake."

Smoke Alarm

Exactly 233 years ago last Wednesday, a firing squad aboard *HMS Monarque* shot Admiral John Byng because he had failed to relieve Minorca. This much we know. History, however, does not record whether the condemned man smoked a hearty valedictory pipeful of rich dark navy shag.

Nor, when, exactly 47 years later, Johann Strauss the Elder was born in Vienna – as yet, of course, not elder than anything, but I am a glutton for meticulousness – do we know whether his father (Johann Strauss the Eldest?) paced the creaking boards outside the birth chamber, chain-smoking those little cheroots upon which, as a publican, he would have had no trouble laying his trembling hands. But it is a fair bet there were big fat thigh-rolled corona-coronas all round when, on the March 14s of both 1820 and 1844, Victor Emmanuel II and his son Umberto I were born (in that order) to a rejoicing Italy. Probably Romeo y Julietas: they are a romantic race.

Harder to say about Albert Einstein, born on March 14, 1879. It was a Friday, and – his father being an orthodox Jew – you would have to know whether Albert popped out before or after sundown had ushered in the fag-forbidding sabbath in order to ponder fruitfully whether the old man had lit up or not. Everything's relative.

Still, even if I had had the hour of Einstein's birth at my fingertips, it would not have stayed there long. Those fingertips are shaking somewhat this evening. That is because this is the evening of March 14, 1990, and the fingertips have had a rough day. They can hardly tap this stuff out. It would be far easier for them if the mouth above them had something dangling from it, but it has had nothing dangling from it for 12 hours and 32 minutes. That is why the brain behind the empty mouth is so preoccupied with other major March 14s, and who might have smoked what on them. For this is the evening of No Smoking Day, and because I have been no-smoking I cannot think about anything else.

I have taken it very seriously. Weeks ago, I made an appointment with a dental hygienist, because this was to be the first morning of the rest of my life, and I wanted to start out with nicotine-free teeth. Also because I was looking for ways of avoiding opportunities to smoke, and once they get a drain in your mouth and a mirror and a little pick-axe, there is no room for a fag.

I managed to get from 7am to 9.30am without screaming at anybody much, although my driving seemed a shade more vocal than usual, but when my coin stuck in the Wimpole Street meter, a number of pinstriped passers-by paused hopefully to watch me kicking it, because, down there, a cardiac arrest can mean serious money.

So can scaling and polishing, if it takes an hour. It takes an hour when there is so much old ochre calculus that the hygienist has to use an ultrasonic chisel. This vibrates at 25,000 somethings a second, and the beam continues until a target interrupts it. It can take tobacco stains off the moon.

I emerged, gums ringing, at 10.45, and strutted down Wimpole Street smiling at windows. Dazzling. No one with teeth like that would ever smoke again. Even if there was a ticket on their windscreen. "It's a test," I said to the car, "the ASH people are jamming the meters of smokers and putting tickets on their windscreens to see if crisis makes them crack and light up." A pin-striped passer-by paused and looked, because, down there, paranoia can mean serious money.

But I did not crack, I left it there and walked to John Lewis, because you are not allowed to smoke in John Lewis, and I bought dental floss and titchy inter-dental brushes; and thence to Ebury Street, to lunch at Mijanou, because they have a no-smoking room, and at 3pm I knew luck was on my side because the cab I hailed thanked me for not smoking. And I got back to my car and ASH had fixed a clamp to the wheel.

I phoned, and they said two hours, and that was the worst time. I crossed the road to Sir Clement Freud's house, because you may not smoke in it, but ASH had sent Sir Clement out of England, so I sat in the car, counting Silk Cut jumping over a stile, but I couldn't sleep.

Nor, back at home, shall I try now. I intend to stay up for the next four hours and, what is it, 12 minutes. I want to be awake when Smoking Day starts.

185

APRIL

This is the Night Mail, Crossing the Border

As of this morning, more precisely as of this dawn, there is a new noise to plague the shallow sleeper. New, at any rate, to me.

I have, over the subsomniac years, grown accustomed to most of the sighs and clicks and grunts and moans and squeaks and mutterings that rise from the no-man's land between sleep and waking, before the Very light arcs upwards from the unscrambling brain to identify their various sources and calm the urban heart ever on the *qui vive* for jemmy and footfall.

I have been nudged from dreams by joists creaking confidentially to one another, and doors unlatching themselves, and radiators tuning up, and sashes nattering irritably at the gale, and I have semi-consciously ticked the noise off the list and slid back, reassured, into sleep. I have heard the fridge wake and juggle loose bottles, briefly, before both of us dropped off again, and cocked an ear to the rasp of little claws on the tiles above my head as early birds hurried, like overdue muezzins, to their choral vantage-points. I have even learned not to be too disquieted by that curious whim

189

of crumpled paper which persuades it suddenly to uncrumple itself in its nocturnal bin for no reason at all.

But, until the small hour just gone, I had not previously been woken by a low spasmodic natter, a tinny insistent buzz simultaneously familiar and unfamiliar, which bothered me for several seconds until familiarity finally prevailed. Two rooms away, my fax machine was going. Someone was sending me something. I groped for my watch, and the lighter which would enable me to read it once I had located the glasses to read it through, and after a bit, when the four of us had convened on the carpet where we had severally fallen, I discovered that it was 5 am.

This was not a noise merely to be added to the list, and immediately ticked off. This was a message, generated, it had to be assumed, by urgency. I rose from the carpet, felt my way out of the bedroom, lurched across the hall towards the chattering fax, and switched on the light. As I did so, the machine stopped, leaving two sheetsworth unspooled from its lip. I tore the paper off; squinted; focused.

"FAXHAM" it said at the top, in large caps.

It had come from Faxham; where was Faxham? Some ghastly grid-streeted New Town custom-created to serve the electronic era, a place of windowless anodized aluminium complexes where time was irrelevant and hard-eyed, unsleeping youths in floral braces and tasselled loafers scuttled day and night between banks of clattering hardware, breaking briefly from their career-paths only for savage bouts of squash and lechery?

I read on, and discovered that Faxham was not this at all. Faxham was not even a place, faxham was a genus. The paragraph dependent from the title explained that the faxham was, cf. the radio ham, a component of a vast network of like-minded enthusiasts, a member of a covert brotherhood, an officer in an élite subversive cadre . . .

In other words, a lonely crackpot who had managed to get his hands on a device capable of trawling the night on the offchance that other lonely crackpots might be seduced into his ghastly fellowship. He had not faxed me specifically, he continued, since he did not know me from Adam – the faxham simply tapped arbitrarily into the void, like a Voyager mission broken free from its solar tether and hoping sometime, somewhere, to encounter responsive life.

It occurred to me, since he had of course left his number, to fax back a curt message pointing out that the way he could know me from Adam was by recalling that Adam was the one able to hide himself even from the Lord God among the trees of the garden, as the result of the Lord God's oversight in failing to provide Adam with a fax machine: but I reflected that I had not been born yesterday. I have learned that not only does a crackpot not require one word of encouragement, one word of discouragement is usually enough to have him grappling himself to you with hoops of steel. Ignore them, is the only course with crackpots.

So I switched the machine off. I looked at it for a bit. The slogan which had drawn me to it in the first place had been: "The world at your fingertips." Of the world's fingertips, nobody had seen fit to say a word.

Wizard Prang

S orry about this. But for fate's googly, you would at this moment have been teetering on the rim of a truly remarkable theory, and poised, your little hand in my big strong one, to plunge into bottomless speculation.

For – sitting in my dawn eyrie and marinating the simultaneous news that a big gun was being bolted together with the object of shooting an Iraqi on the surface of Mars, that seven prisoners had legged it out of Gloucester chokey by shinning down knotted sheets, that the Japanese were about to produce a ship capable of travelling at 100 knots by virtue of giant magnets, that the Hungarian army had recorded an encounter at Tarnaszentmaria barracks with giant extra-terrestrial creatures, and that a spokesman for young snookerperson Allison Fisher had declared that the only course now open to her was to infiltrate the circuit disguised as a bloke – it had suddenly occurred to me that the world was currently being organized by a couple of mischievous old hacks formerly employed by *The Wizard*. How they had got their hands on the world was not immediately apparent, but it was probably something to do with a secret formula they had stumbled across in an old Egyptian tomb and handed to the mad professor in their basement.

Sadly, I have been unable to pursue this to what would have been our mutual satisfaction. For, just as I was musing on exactly how long it might be before Mr Nicholas Ridley confessed that the bits of guttering recently shipped to Guam were indeed parts of a giant seebackascope, or that the true reason behind Vivian Richards's extraordinary outburst at Sabina Park was that a small boy in the crowd had succeeded not only in imitating the great man's voice but also in throwing it 200 yards, a blackbird – almost certainly from Porlock – flew past my dormer and drove all such trains of thought into a blind siding.

The bird had a twig in its mouth; but not for long. As it alighted on the branch opposite my window, it dropped the twig. It looked down for a bit. Then it hopped over to a little heap of similar twigs and began beaking it furiously. Several of these twigs now fell out of the tree. The blackbird stared at what was left. Then it flew off.

I opened the sash, and leaned out for a closer peer. When I say that a nest was under construction, I should not like anyone to be misled: the pitiful little pile stood in roughly the same relationship to the usual beak-woven miracle as a builder's skip does to Blenheim Palace. Most of the aggregate had no chance whatever of incorporation into a successful billet: there were sweetpapers here, bits of flex, a couple of corks, a wizened daffodil, and even the twigs were of obviously grossly incompatible girth. It was as if the blackbird were firing on half-instinct – some arcane force had urged it to begin collecting stuff, but left it with not the remotest idea of why it was being collected.

The bird flew back. It had a little red lid with it, possibly a Smartie cap. It put it on the pile. It flew off again. The heart went out. This bird was in real trouble. Did it know what it was building wasn't a nest? Would it eventually bring a female back to this wobbling heap, stick her on it, expect gratitude, get a beak in its eye? Worse, would it bring back an equally dim female (nature has a way of peer-bonding), and would she deposit her eggs on the mound only to have them roll off? I saw the parents gazing down at their family beneath, sunny side up, and I was riven.

What should one do? Let nature take its course, or intervene? The garden is full of old nests, I could ladder one up, crawl along the . . .

I stopped there. Monitory neck-hairs had risen, just in time. *Dopey Old Birdsnester Gets Come-Uppance as Limb Snaps* ran the headline in my brain. Used to happen all the time, in *The Wizard*.

My Heart's in the Highlands

Remove my trousers and stroll the public streets? Yes, without a second thought, when longevity is the prize. For the days grow short as you reach September, and if all it takes to lengthen them is a touch of nether nakedness, a man would be a fool to persist with homicidal worsted. Especially as the alternative is herring.

Even more especially as I had spent a glum Saturday believing that it was in fact to the herring that no alternative was offered. For, as fellow-valetudinarians will need no reminding, the morning had brought the ambivalent news that a diet of herring had been proved to reduce the odds against coronary clog-popping by some 30 per cent. I cannot stand herring, but since I can stand even less the prospect of keeling over before 2018, and thus never seeing a dividend from my Euro-tunnel shares, I had all but come to terms with the idea of the house's henceforth smelling like the Pequod, when, the following dawn, *The Sunday Times* thumped to the mat.

Where, beneath the headline, *Cure For Heart Disease*, I discovered – making my own burst into a disconcertingly arhythmic clatter – that a Dr Malcolm Carruthers had delivered a lecture to Edinburgh's Lister Institute anent the astonishing cardiac benefits of the kilt. Since I do not enjoy the franchise to shock which goes with Dr Carruthers's qualifications, I shall not detail the unsavoury biochemistry involved, except to say that it is all to do with airflow round

194

what the medical profession calls Down There, and its beneficial effect on the production of testosterone. I do not know what testosterone is, but it is apparently even better for the heart than herring, and you do not have to cut its head off and poke it down the waste-disposal.

All I needed further to know, therefore, was whether I could wear the kilt. I do not mean whether I *might*, for while, admittedly, few indeed are the Corens wha hae wi' Wallace bled, there is one tartan which is permitted to all and that is the Hunting Stuart. Although even the St Andrew's Woollen Mill, arbiter of all things tartan, did not know why this should be, it confirmed, when I rang, that anyone might indeed wear with impunity this natty green, red, and yellow item: which, furthermore, they would be happy to provide upon receipt of my measurement from navel to knee, and 170, if I heard aright, poonds.

So I might; but *could* I? It would make sense, surely, before filling an envelope with poonds, to find out whether I could dredge up the requisite nerve to walk abroad (which is what Cricklewood would instantly become if I did). I therefore presented myself at Bermans & Nathans Ltd, theatrical costumiers of Camden Town, and within the hour stood girt not merely in a rented kilt, but in sporran, Highland jacket, waistcoat, brogues, and socks sporting those little green tabs I had last worn to complement a woggle.

I say stood, because that is exactly what I did, for some time. I had parked my car outside Bermans, but I did not know how to get into it. Then a woman drew up in a Golf and asked if I was going, and I said she could have the parking place in return for a little information, and she said what you do is sit down first and then swing your legs in together, and it worked, more or less, and a strange sensation it was, after 40 years of putting one leg in first.

But everything was all right, after that. Instead of the anticipated derision, I have for the past three days met only that extraordinary politeness which comes when people are studiously avoiding noticing something. I am a joke which

195

nobody dares make. They go out of their way to be solicitous, they usher me towards counters at which they are queuing, they come up to me in the street, if I pause for the merest moment, and ask me if I am lost. Furthermost, I am a social catalyst: from the corner of my eye, I see strangers begin to talk to one another when they think I can't see that it's me they're talking about.

All of which places a heavy incumbency upon me. I dare not let them down, they must not twig I am not as I seem; so I cannot speak to them. I find myself grunting, a pastime entirely novel to me. I have become A Man of Few Words. Sassenachs doubtless see me as a typical Scottish misery.

It would never occur to them that the heart has its reasons.

Prose and Cons

See the spring in my step! Note the light in my eye! Clock the chuckle playing about my lips: what can he be bringing us this morning, you ask?

Good news to all who fear that the art of letter-writing is dead, is what.

It is a big all, else I should not bother to bring it. Indeed, such flies fortunate enough to have been left on the walls of middle-class dinner parties after the Filipino has been round with the Flit will readily testify that the talk is often of little else. You know, I'm sure, the scene: quickly mopped up with the watercress soup have been the Heseltine anabasis, the Gooch fracture and the Gorbachov dichotomy; the

196

unhealthy dominance of mytho-genetic fiction and the tendency of the 3-series to oversteer in the wet have got us through the marinated hake, and here we are, staring gloomily at our kumquat sorbets and lamenting that nobody writes letters any more.

This is all down, we mutter, to electronic prostheses. From here on in it will be *Lord Chesterfield's Carphone Calls To His Son, The Collected Faxes of Elizabeth Barrett Browning,* and Edmund Burke's *Answering Machine Message to a Noble Lord on the Attacks made upon him and his Pension in the House of Lords by the Duke of Bedford and the Earl of Lauderdale.*

So choked do we become at this drear prospect that by the time the crown of lamb heaves to alongside, we can hardly bring ourselves to address the threat of the Teutonic revival.

Well, phooey, I say. I say it not lightly, but with the full confidence of one who – following a trade which admittedly leaves him, perhaps, more time on his hands than you – actually reads all the unsolicited mail which clogs his porch, and who always believed that, some day, the junk would bring forth the man. Well, the day dawned this morning. The man works for the Maestros Bodegueros of Madrid. The junk is art.

His letter has the most compelling opening in all Spanish literature (and no, I have not forgotten "At a certain village in La Mancha, which I shall not name, there lived not long ago one of those old-fashioned gentlemen who are never without a lance upon a rack, an old target, a lean horse and a greyhound"). The letter begins:

"Dear Mr Coren. Some of the most important winemaking families in Spain have entrusted me to write to you on their behalf."

Do we not see it all in that brilliantly economical *entrusted?* The cloaked cabal convened beneath the cellar's flickering flambeaux, the plangent pluck of flamenco from the bodega above, the long agonized debate in low hoarse voices, and, at last, Sr Segundo Sanz (for it is he) selected by secret ballot to commit to vellum the quill which will save them all. A wise choice. Sr Sanz has style. More yet: when epistolary duty's to be done, Sr Sanz has *aficion*.

"They have asked me to explain why we are inviting you to purchase the beautiful wines we produce. Yet they are afraid that you may believe this is yet another sales letter inspired by the commercial pressures which now pervade our once gentlemanly business."

How could I believe that? Or fail to believe anything of a man who writes "You need not pay until you receive the wines, for the people of Britain are an honest people"? We know Sr Sanz is not in it for the money, he is in it for the words. Would that I had room here to select more of the thousand he has written, the mellifluous evocation of the lunch at which our own dear Queen sipped their *Marques de Alella*, the shimmering tropes devoted to the great mansions beneath which proud Spanish aristocrats stroll gazing raptly at their Maestros Bodegueros stocks, the wondrous depiction of "the children of the vineyard" as they spoonfeed each swelling pip – you will just have to believe me when I say that, as far as the Latin renaissance is concerned, García Márquez and Fuentes and Casares and Allende and Vargas Llosa may be all very well over the distance, but they will have to get the whip out sharpish if they are not to be trounced by Segundo in the sprint.

This afternoon I shall write to him, not because I want his wine, but because I want another letter. I tell you, my forthcoming edition of *The Collected Junkmail of Segundo Sanz* is going to be something very special.

The Cricklewood Hop

At 95p, there can be no bigger bargain on God's earth than a frog. Or, indeed, on God's water. Which is perhaps the most remarkable feature of all: for not only after you slap down your sovereign do you receive, in addition to a bob in change, something which hops, croaks and mops up flies – each function alone astonishing value for the money – you walk away with that incredible item, an amphibian, equally at home on log or ripple. You can take a frog anywhere.

Compare this with the cheapest goldfish on the market. At £1.85, you are buying little more than a lacquered minnow. It does not hop, it does not croak, and if you put it on a log, it will pop its finny clogs. Furthermore, not only does it not eat flies, it requires the regular sustenance of Bioflakes at £3.99 a pot, because if it is not waited on hand and foot with its daily 21.5 per cent protein, 5.2 per cent fibre, 11.8 per cent minerals, and vitamins A, D and E, it will turn over on its back.

The only consolation to watching £1.85 go belly-up is that it is probably the most interesting thing the goldfish will ever do. I have never been able to understand why people put goldfish in their ponds: I can just about discern the case for putting them in an aquarium, where they will at least glare at you, but the only time you ever see them in a pond is when they come up briefly to make a hole in £3.99. As soon as they have got 21.5 per cent protein inside them, they

199

disappear again. Whatever they find to stare at down there under the weeds, it is not you.

Now, readers with uncluttered memories may recall that I reached these conclusions a whole year ago when I sought to stock my pond with more substantial fauna than the newts, snails and little squiggly things which had hitherto held ecological sway beside the rockery. Wishing to do things right in a neighbourhood lazily committed to bedder and sapling, I planted frogs from seed: a big bucket of spawn went in, and in due season several hundred tadpoles graduated from the maternal jelly and began growing. They also, such is the way with evolution, began vanishing; indeed, the relationship between the growing and the vanishing proceeded at so apparently symbiotic a rate that I could not but conclude that brother was gobbling brother, until that moment when I caught one of the last giant survivors disappearing head-first into a newt.

Which is why last Saturday found me strolling the humid aisles of Wilding's Pond Centre. This is not unlike an aquatic Reeperbahn: from tank after seductive tank a hitherto unimaginable array of freshwater delights ogles and suppli-cates, inviting the unbuttoned wallet to take them home to do their thing. There are umpteen varieties of fish, from orfe the size of airgun darts to catfish so enormous as to suggest they are named not for their physiognomy but their diet; there are countless breeds of newt and toad and axolotl and other exotica so expensive you would swear they had been raised from caviare ...and down at the rough end of town there are common frogs at 95p apiece.

I bought a bagful. Half a dozen. In the car, they sat on the seat beside me; when I stopped on The Ridgeway to glean a chunk of log, I could hear them croaking. They missed me already.

Back home, I put the log in the pond, and the frogs on the log. They did everything right. They hopped off it. They climbed back on. They paddled about. They croaked again. I felt like God. I had made a world.

They did their stuff throughout that sunny afternoon. In

200

the evening I went out to dinner, and when I came home at midnight I nipped out to see how they were getting on.

I tiptoed through the grass and shone my torch. They were not in the pond. They were climbing the rockery. Caught in the searchlight beam, they froze. It was like Colditz. Had they planned to send me a postcard when they got to Switzerland?

What should I do, at this point where nature met nurture? Interfere with the Great Scheme of Things? What would God do? Dumb question – as far as God is concerned, £5.70 is neither here nor there. Gently, I plucked them from their flight and put them back on the log. On Sunday, I put a net over the pond.

Bloody amphibians. You may be able to take a frog anywhere, but keeping it there turns out to be a very different kettle of fish.

Uncool Water

Those of you who have sat outside the gates of Wormwood Scrubs with the meter running, gnawing a thumbnail and pondering your future relationship with the loved one ambling sheepishly through the dawn towards you in his dated flares and crepe-soled brogues, his brown-paper bundle held out as if in pitiful propitiation, will understand my state of mind this morning.

Fraught is the nexus of emotions I am struggling to unravel. I am enwebbed by reflections on crime and punishment, on loyalty and betrayal, on disfavour and rehabilitation, on affection and rejection. For something once close to me has returned, and it has been through hell, but my arms have not opened as wide as either of us would wish.

Perrier has been doing time. It has been banged up. Caught with its hand in the benzene, it has been paying its debt to society. Furthermore, in consequence of that debt, it has been having itself sorted out. Behind the crenellated walls, the caring society has been at it. It has been doctored. It now wears a little bottle-badge which reads "New production", though it is gamely trying to bear the stigma with pride. In full-page press ads and television commercials, it is winsomely murmuring "Helleau again". It is, in short, asking for the forgiveness it has done everything in its power to justify. It is trying to persuade me to give it another chance.

But shall I grant it? I ask because I have just come back from the off-licence, where, sprung only this morning from chokey, Le Perrier Nouveau was sitting expectantly on the shelf, yet what I have come back with is Highland Spring. Not because I hold any brief for Highland Spring, nor for Badoit, nor yet for Malvern, Evian, Volvic, or anything else with which I have been knocking about while Perrier was doing its bird, but simply because absence makes the heart grow fickle, and promiscuity breeds indiscrimination. If it bubbles, these days, it'll do.

I lie, even to myself. It is a characteristic of the unfaithful. If I think about it honestly, I am forced to recognize that for some time before the tragedy at Vergeze I had been looking for an excuse to part the ways with Perrier. I know the signs, now. I have been there before, and more than once. Call them mineral watersheds.

Until I was 12, I drank Tizer. It was what boys did. It went with the conker, the slow-worm, and the tie beneath the ear. Most important of all, it was disapproved of by parents. It made you belch. Parents wanted you to drink barley water. Barley water cleansed the blood.

At puberty, the macho image that accompanied filthy

blood would no longer do. Nor were eructations that dislodged masonry enough. If you took a girl to the Moo Cow Milk Bar and ordered two Tizers, that was the end of it. You had to break it off with Tizer. You had to order Coke. Coke was adult. Coke was American. Coke was nearly as good as having a Chevy. Coke was nearly as good as the real thing.

Until you were 18. If you were 18 and you took a girl to the Rat & Cockle and ordered two Cokes, that was the end of it. You had to break it off with Coke. You had to order tonic. It had to have gin in it. G&TS were nearly as good as having a Jensen. G&TS were nearly as good as playing backgammon. For the next 20 years, you fell over a lot.

Your afternoons did not stabilize until the late 1970s, when, if you took a girl to the White Elephant and ordered two G&TS, that was the end of it. G&TS meant a fat gut and a maraschino eye and gasping during the real thing. You had to break it off with G&TS. You had to order Perrier. Perrier was nearly as good as having a Ferrari. Perrier stated that you did not wish to jeopardize your squash rating. Perrier was keeping you in shape for the real thing. Perrier said you had a window around 4 pm.

And then, when you were a little older still, you heard yourself, one day, ordering Perrier, and it came to you that you had been drinking things for the wrong reasons for too long, and that the time was past when dashes needed cutting. You had to break it off with Perrier.

But somehow you never did. Perhaps because it was the last link in the chain. And then they caught it red-handed. They broke it off for you.

"Eau revoir," you cried loyally, in the wake of the departing paddy-waggon. But in your heart you knew it was really cheerieau.

MAY

Book Now, Pay Later

I have managed to locate Twin Falls, Idaho, in my atlas. It is just up the road from Glens Ferry, and just down the road from Blackfoot. Or, more accurately, up and down the river from them, because Twin Falls lies at the southern extremity of the Snake River Plain, straddling its eponym. It has Shoshone to the north, and Riddle to the west, and Sosa Springs to the east, and Grouse Creek to the south.

It thus sounds as small-town American as it is possible to be, and these sounds interfere ineluctably with my vision of it.

If you say those names aloud, Norman Rockwell paints their landscape in your head. You see picket fences and clapboard houses and yellow pick-up trucks and children in plaid mackinaws and ear-muffs throwing snowballs, and beaming men in armbands and half-moon spectacles peering out at them from behind the windows of the Twin Falls Savings & Loan. These men are waiting for James Stewart to come in and offer them plangent homilies and boxes of home-tied trout flies in exchange for yet another extension to his mortgage, and they will accept, for that is the kind of small town this is.

Or sounds to be. Who can tell with names? To the untravelled American, Milton Keynes doubtless conjures up a picture of some idyllic spot where Bloomsberries loll around spouting epic pentameters at one another. It could be that Twin Falls is an industrial tip, a junky ashram, a missile site. It may enjoy the highest murder rate in America.

Why do I need to know? I need to know because Twin Falls is where Charles P. Wincott lives, and I need to envisage Charles P. Wincott in his domestic environment. But I cannot even envisage Charles P. Wincott. I do, mind, have a slightly less fuzzy image of him than you do, because I know one thing about him you don't. When you hear his name, it is quite likely that an image materializes of a rather formal Twin Falls citizen: the bank manager, perhaps, the editor of *The Twin Falls Picayune*, even the mayor.

You do not know that he is nine years old. I do, because he has written to me, signing himself "Charles P. Wincott (aged 9)" in a big round pencil script.

Now, when you write chidren's books, you reap a special whirlwind: the readers write back. Many of them write back even when they don't want to, because they have been forced to read your book in class, and part of the exercise is to write to the author and make him regret the day he didn't go into dentistry or fish-farming.

American schools are a particular headache on this score, because whole classes write, and often they write the same letter, since this is the way their teacher has pointed them, e.g. "Arthur is on a horse on page 16 but he is not on it on page 23, where has the horse gone or is this a mistake, please write as soon as possible."

You are then stuck with writing 26 individual letters to Alopecia, Wis., at a mailing cost of a tenner, because if you don't they all think you're a rat, and the school board will not buy any more of your books.

Since they would have to buy 100 of them for you just to get the tenner back, this is a lousy deal, but you do it anyway, because *you* don't want to think you're a rat, either.

And also because the occasional incoming letter lets it be known that the sender wants to be a writer, too, and asks questions about how to get started and where do the ideas come from and do you use a pen or a typewriter, and although the odds are long against their ever cracking it, you feel an incumbency to keep their spirits up, because you might thus stop one or two of them from going into dentistry or fish-farming.

But the truth is, the questions they ask are never the right ones. At least they weren't until Charle P. Wincott came along. I opened his letter yesterday, and I quote his final paragraph in full:

"I want to be a writer, and what I would like to know is how much did you make last year, what car do you drive, and do you have a boat and a beach-house?"

Which is why I need a clear picture both of Charles P. Wincott and of Twin Falls, Idaho. For I rather feel the world will be hearing more of him, and of it, and I want to be able to say I knew them when.

Rough Diamond

As I type, the gypsy ring on my third finger, right hand, jiggles. After a hundred words or so, the weight of its solitaire diamond will have turned the ring back to front. The ring will have shuffled around my finger, leaving the diamond on the palm side. It will do this because it is a big heavy diamond, and the ring is slightly too large for my finger.

I do not know why it is called a gypsy ring. It is not the kind of ring you see on gypsies. Were a doorstep bunch of lucky white heather to be shoved in your face, the hand bunching it would not have a ring like this on it. A ring like this is a lousy marketing feature if you are begging door-to-door: the shank contains so much gold, that when you put it on, your hand drops to your side. Were I a frailer man, I should walk with a list.

Not only is it not a gypsy's ring, it is not a hack's ring, either. I know a lot of writers, and I have never seen a ring like this on any of them. I saw Freddie Forsyth notice it once, and after he had noticed it, he shot his cuff over his wrist, because his Rolex Oyster wasn't in the same league. Jeffrey Archer clocked it and said "Where did you get that?" and I have never known him put that question to anyone else, because his researchers can generally be counted on to find out all about anything, and for a man like Jeffrey to do his own asking means that this is a very special ring indeed.

It is the ring of an almost-villain. A ducker-and-diver, a man who does a bit of this and a bit of that. The manager of a couple of iffy middleweights, perhaps, or the proprietor of three gravel pits and a health club which keeps changing addresses. It is a ring which gives every impression of having been bought with dodgy notes by someone who had to launder money fast.

And a hard man, too. It is a ring which adds a good few ounces to the fist; it suggests that were you to get on the wrong side of its owner, and were he to be standing between you and the door, then you might find yourself in what men with rings like this call a situation.

If you are a hack, however, and you wear a ring like this while you are hacking, it does something to your style. Days when I wear it, I use a lot less syllables and I don't call them fewer syllables. If Hemingway had been a gypsy, I would know why this was called a gypsy ring.

Why, then, have I got it? I have got it because it is an heirloom. A year ago, two days before my old man died (if I were not wearing the ring when I typed that, I would have called him my father), he took his hand out from under the hospital blanket and asked me to take the ring off, because he was running out of energy and the ring had been on his finger a long time. We both had to tug a bit, but then it came off, and I put it on. As rites of passage go, you would be pressed to find neater.

My old man was not dodgy. He was hard, but he was not dodgy. It was his father-in-law who was dodgy, and also hard; he was so hard that when he died he left the ring to my father rather than to his own son, because his own son was dodgier than anybody, and the ring would have been hocked before my maternal grandfather's box had dropped the full distance. Both my maternal grandfather and his son were gamblers, and they always owed people money, but whereas the people didn't come after my grandfather because he would have thumped them, they always came after my uncle, because he would get hold of something to hock, and pay up. That was what my grandfather hated about him most of all.

So I have the ring now; but am I hard and dodgy enough for it? Yesterday, I went to have it valued for probate, because I forgot to mention it last year, and the noise I heard as I walked in was my old man's old-man-in-law spinning in his grave at the thought of grandfathering someone who worried about conning the Probate Office.

"It's a big stone," said the man with the thing in his eye. "Worth five thousand, if it was any good."

"Isn't it any good?" I said.

"It has a horrible flaw," he said.

"But a lot of gold," I observed.

"A lot of nine-carat gold," he said. "I'll put it down for £100."

"Don't bother," I said, and I took it back, and walked out.

You would have shrunk to the wall as I passed. Here was a man prepared to conceal £100 from the Probate Office. Hard, you would have said, dodgy.

211

You Can't Be Sirius

One of the compensations – one, indeed, of the considerable reliefs – of what we shall call middle maturity is that you cease testing yourself. You no longer deliberately confront the hitherto unconfronted in order to discover what sort of person you are. This is partly because you have found out almost all there is to find out, partly because you have better things to do with the diminishing time remaining than to winkle out the few things you do not know and put scalpel and litmus to them, and partly because you also have better things to do with the diminishing time remaining than to act upon the information received.

Then somebody buys you a telescope.

Nobody who is bought a telescope says, "Hallo, a telescope", and leaves it in the box in case it spells trouble. He opens the box. He takes out all the gleaming enamelled tubes and the glittering brass fitments and the winking blued lenses, and he begins fitting them together. He takes out the anodized tripod, and he screws its sturdy black rubber feet on, and he spanners the bracing struts into place, and he sets it up and fits the telescope to it, and upon the sixth hour he stands back and looks at the work that he has done, and finds it good. He rests from his labours with a large one. He walks around the telescope, so that, from any angle, he may congratulate himself on being the sort of man who can put together a complicated thing like a telescope.

And he does not once, during all this, ask himself if he is the sort of man who looks through them. Even though he has always maintained that there are two sorts of people who look through things, and that the sorts they are are determined by the sort of things through which they look.

There are binocular men and there are telescope men.

Binocular men are extrovert, outdoor, tough, racy, dominant and decisive. In a crisis, the man with binoculars round his neck puts them to his eyes, comes to an instant conclusion, and acts upon it. He may do this from the top of the Goodwood stands, or from the turret of a Tiger tank, or from just below the South Col of Everest, or even from a big cardboard box on Romney Marsh. But whether he is bent on determining if the second favourite is to be backed, or the attack to commence from the left flank, or the assault on the summit to be made before the weather closes in, or merely if the thing hopping about in his lenses is greater or lesser spotted, determine it he will, because that is what he does.

Telescope men, on the other hand, are introvert, indoor, meek, dull, biddable, and dithering. They sit in the loft, with one eye shut, wondering what it is that the other eye is seeing. Is that Betelgeuse? Concorde? A gnat on the lens? They entertain theories about black holes and red dwarfs, but with scant conviction. They wonder about how it all started, what it is doing now, and where it will all end; but they will not commit themselves.

Now, into which category have I spent my life imagining I fell? Of course. Furthermore, apart from all that, I have never had the slightest interest in the heavens. I am one of those solipsists who, strolling out on to a nocturnal terrace and gazing up at the blackness's billion punctuation points, suddenly has borne in upon him how insignificant *they* are. I have never recognized any of them from their photographs. I have, of course, long known that there is a collection which looks like a saucepan, but on the nights when, for some reason, it hasn't seemed to be there, it has never bothered me in the slightest.

But look at me now. This is my third midnight in the loft.

213

That is a bottle of Volnay. Those are cheddar sandwiches. The big fat book is *The Times Atlas of the Universe*. We are all waiting for things to rise, but the big fat book is the only one who knows what those things are. The rest of us are equally in the dark; although, on reflection, I cannot speak for the cheddar, which is full of bacteria that may have some innate sense regarding star movements.

The curious – and unnerving – thing is that it doesn't matter when I peer through the telescope, the stars are scarcely larger than they are with the naked eye, and yet I cannot stop looking at them. I do not know why this should be. All I know is that I have been put through a test I should have preferred not to have taken. I have, probably with everything which this entails, become a telescope man.

A Prawn in the Game

There is a prawn on my shoe.

The man on my right is rabbiting on captivatingly about the threat of the core curriculum to all we have and hold, and the woman on my left is being no less fascinating about the gratuitous degradation of slopping-out, and my head is swivelling sociably between the two and giving every appearance of bi-polar commitment, but what it is really thinking about is the prawn on my shoe.

One of the many things it is thinking about the prawn on my shoe is whether the people to its left and right are also thinking about the prawn on my shoe. I have not noticed them glancing down, but when I turn to the woman on my

214

left, how can I be sure that the man on my right is not staring at my toecap?

For that is where the prawn is. When I say it is on my shoe, I do not mean I have trodden it on to my sole, I mean I am concentrating on not treading it on to my sole, which is what could very well happen if it dislodges itself from my toecap. If that were to happen, it would flatten itself on to my host's magnificent Bokhara rug. That would do the magnificent Bokhara rug no good at all.

I am still holding the outer wall of the vol-au-vent case from which the prawn recently fell. Soon after I took the vol-au-vent from the proffered tray, its floor fell out, and the prawn fell after it. I did not know this had happened, because I was engaged in the core curriculum debate at the time, and it seemed rude to sink my teeth into the vol-au-vent while the bloke was talking, so I held it for a bit, and when a pause allowed me to turn to the woman on my left, the plan was to bite the vol-au-vent as I swivelled, which was when I noticed that the floor had fallen out, and that the prawn was no longer there. I glanced down, and I saw it on my shoe.

It is a suede shoe, which gives maximum adhesion to a fallen prawn, especially when the prawn has goo on it. The goo is a mixed blessing: with average luck, it will keep the prawn on my toecap while I sidle somewhere private and remove it, but if I hang about, the goo will do the suede no good at all. You know suede.

You will ask why I do not bend quickly and pluck the prawn off. That is because I have not explained that this is Sunday morning at a house where the rooms, though delightful, are not quite large enough for the huge number of charming folk who have convened for drinks, so that we are all packed nose to chin, with, moreover, fully occupied hands. I have a glass in one, and the remains of a vol-au-vent in the other. In order to pluck the prawn off my toecap, I should have to ask either the man on my right – who is now in full spate on the outrageous excision of English Literature from the syllabus – to hold my glass, or the woman on my left – who is now addressing the matter of four men occupying a cell originally designed for one – to hold my vol-au-vent case.

I should then have to sort of concertina myself downwards, thereby drawing considerable attention to what I was attempting covertly to go down after. And even if nobody saw what I was going down after, they would unquestionably see what I came up with. I should have a prawn in my hand.

I shall just have to excuse myself and walk out of the room, very carefully. I am doing that now, smiling at people so that they will not look down and wonder why this man is limping about with a prawn on his shoe. I am on the stairs now, and the prawn is going up and down very gingerly, as the pair of us look for a lavatory so that one of us can put down the glass and the vol-au-vent case and throw the other one down the pan.

I have found the lavatory. I have taken the prawn from my toecap, and pulled the chain.

I have looked into the pan to make sure the prawn has gone. I have made sure it hasn't. It is circling gently on the surface. It did not occur to me that that is what prawns do, alive or dead. They are hydrodynamic.

I have come quickly out of the lavatory now, and look who is smiling at me and waiting to come in! It is my host. When he sees the prawn, what will he wonder? Who can say?

I know only what I shall wonder. I shall wonder whether I prefer to be remembered as a guest who threw his food down the lavatory to one who trod it into the carpet; and I shall probably wonder it for quite a long time.

Ping-

D ressing was the first huidle. I had not gone as freight before. I did not know how freight dressed.

I kept walking to the window and looking at the hired furniture-van at the kerb, attempting to imagine official reaction to seeing it drive up with a brown trilby at the wheel. And a green tweed jacket below the trilby, and a yellow tie bisecting the jacket. A monocle, even.

Then I walked around the room for a while, and went back to the window and attempted to imagine official reaction to seeing it drive up with a flat cap at the wheel. And blue dungarees below the flat cap. No tie. A string vest, perhaps. A bare hairy elbow resting on the sill. Possibly an unlit dog-end gummed to the lower lip.

None of this, you understand, had anything to do with van etiquette or even simple aesthetics; what it had everything to do with was credibility. Unfortunately, I did not know I should need credibility until it was too late to do anything about it except attempt to imagine.

The night before we were to envan for France, the know-all we were having dinner with inquired whether I had a consular tampon on my manifest.

I looked at him for a bit.

I may have said, "What manifest?"

He may have looked at his wife. Mine may have looked at me. After I had swallowed the ashes in my mouth, I said that I was simply driving a vanload of our old furniture to the

217

south of France to give the French woodworm we had recently bought something to think about, and that nobody had said anything about a manifest, and what was all that about tampons?

Whereupon he explained, reasonably unsmugly all things considered, all the things I had not considered; prime among which were the facts that all freight entering France requires a contents manifest and that this manifest needs to be signed by the French consul in London, testifying that it is free of all duties, imposts, and English woodworm who might precipitate an international incident were they suddenly to come across their French counterparts in the middle of a table-leg. A *tampon* is a rubber stamp the French consul keeps on his desk which proves that he is the French consul.

"Well, you'll just have to bluff it out," said my friend. "You know, look the part."

But which part?

Catsmeat Potter-Purbright, monoglot dingbat poppin' down to Antibes with Aunt Agatha's chattels, what-ho, old customs bean, no compree parleyvoo?

Bob Hoskins, professional Bermondsey *routier*, done 40 trips this year, no one said nuffink about no bleeding manifest before, don't ask me, sunshine, phone head office up Ilford?

William Bunter, Owl of the Removal, my manifest blew out of the window, sir, my manifest is in the post, ow, leggo my ear you beastly frog?

"A grey suit?" said my wife, 10 minutes before the off. "You're going to drive a thousand miles in a grey three-piece suit?"

"The French respect formality," I said. "Front up in bespoke English worsted, they are putty in your hands. As soon as we're through the Calais customs, I'll change."

A doddle. They did not even look at the passports. They saluted the suit. The sun came out. I pulled over just before the autoroute, got into jeans and T-shirt, drove through the *péage*, plucked my ticket, and with all Gaul poised for division by my throttle-foot, stopped.

218

You do that when a blue uniform is standing in front of you with its white glove up. When the glove beckons, you pull over, and when it holds itself out you drop your keys in it.

The policeman walked round to the back and I got out and walked round after him, and while he was unlocking the doors, a second policeman walked round after both of us, and hove to. Did I, he wondered, have goods to declare? Might he inspect my manifest?

Mrs Coren looked out of the for'ard window.

"Shall I," she said, "distract their attention while you get back in the suit?"

-Pong

*T*he farrago so far. An Englishman who failed to have *his head examined has arrived in France with a vanload of his old furniture. He has been stopped at the Calais* péage *by two policemen who wish to see the import licence he has not got. Because he has not got it, they wish to see the old furniture. We left them opening the doors. Ten seconds have passed; you may now read on. (All conversation has been roughly translated from the even rougher original.)*

"Lo, the old furniture!" I said.

219

They craned towards the loosely piled chairs, tables, sofas, rugs, pictures and boxfuls of odds and sods. Given the pitiability of all such deracinated stuff, I could not see how their hearts could fail to melt. Homelessness is ever poignant, even in a kettle.

"This is not for sale?"

"How could it be?" I cried. "It is all old. And I am not a merchant of furniture. Lo, my passport."

They ignored it. Instead they climbed inside and began poking about. One sat on a sofa. I prayed it would bong. It had always bonged before. If it bonged now, we should all laugh about broken-down old springs and clap one another upon the shoulder and I should be on my way.

But it did not bong now. It liked Cricklewood. It would miss its friend, the gateleg table. It wanted revenge.

"It is leather?" said the *flic*.

"Of a kind," I said. "But see how creased and worn it is."

"It is antique?"

"No," I cried. "Just old. Broken. Worthless."

Venom came off the sofa. You could taste it.

They convened at a desk; one ran his hand over it, unnecessarily lovingly. This is *The Antique Autoroute Show*, I thought; he is going to ask me if I have any idea of what a remarkable piece like this would fetch at Sotheby's.

"I'm afraid the leg wobbles," I said, with one of those light laughs you only ever seem to hear in customs halls.

He leaned heavily on the desk; the leg did not wobble. "Cricklewood," creaked the desk softly to the sofa.

His colleague eased the wrapping from a picture. It was a Bill Tidy.

"It is an original?"

"It is a cartoon," I said. Did you know that there are two words for cartoon in French? *Carton* means a Leonardo. *Dessin* means a Bill Tidy. It's amazing the things you can find out from a *gendarme*, especially after a long hysterical explanation to the effect that Bill Tidy is alive and well in Solihull, thinks that the Quattrocento is a small Fiat, and knocks out a dozen of these a day.

220

But it was all right. They sucked their teeth, they sniffed, but they finally conceded that none of this stuff was going to destabilize the French fine art market. They were about to hop down again when one casually lifted a dust-sheet, and paused.

"It is new, this table of ping-pong?" he said.

"No," I said, "it is ten years old."

"It has the air of the new," said the copper. "Let us descend it."

They descended it to the road, and set it up. We might have been in one of those short, grainy Czech films: *Two Policemen and a Ping-Pong Table*. Passing drivers gazed. "What is this that this is?" you felt them mutter. A charity match? Avis Vans *v*. La Sûreté, saving the whale?

"It is simply that we have never used it," I explained, but they shook their heads and opened one of those fat, ring-bound books common to all customs men wherein everything is writ concerning dues, attachments and proscriptions anent chiming barometers, vivarium decor, funnel-paint and hatbands (feathered). This they thumbed for some time.

But, miraculously, tables (ping-pong) had no entry. You could anchor a tanker off Brest and unload 10 million tables (ping-pong) with equanimity. So they ascended it again. They nodded brusquely. I climbed back into the cab.

"Good game?" said Mrs Coren.

I watched them dwindle in my mirror. Each was scribbling furiously.

"I have the feeling," I said, "that the last duty-free ping-pong table has just entered France."